WALL STREET KITCHEN

WALL STREET KITCHEN

The Recipe Behind a
Housewife's 1000% Stock Return

VICTOR CHIU

Copyright © 2016 by Victor Chiu. All rights reserved.

Published by Victor Chiu, Vancouver, British Columbia, Canada.

PERMISSIONS: This publication is protected by the Canadian Copyright Act and the Universal Copyright Convention (UCC). It may not be reproduced in part or in whole, nor transmitted or stored by any means, on paper, digitally or any other format, except as expressly permitted by the Canadian Copyright Act, R.S.C., 1985, c. C-42, without obtaining permission in advance by the author. Please address all permission requests to the author at victorchiu.investor@gmail.com.

DISCLAIMER: Both the publisher and author have made their best efforts to ensure accuracy and completeness when preparing this book. However, neither the publisher nor the author make warranties as to the accuracy or completeness of its contents beyond the efforts they have made. Further, no warranty may be invented by any advertising or sales representatives or related documentation, on paper, digitally or any other format. Both the publisher and author warn that the strategies, tactics and advice contained in this book might or might not be appropriate for each reader's individual situation; reader discretion is advised. Should you have any questions as to the appropriateness of any strategies, tactics and advice to your situation, consulting a professional is appropriate. All strategies, tactics and advice contained in this book are to be used at your own risk. The author makes no claims to be a professional financial advisor; all content is based on personal observation, personal experience and research. Neither the publisher nor the author imply that the content of this book constitutes professional financial advice, and readers should not construe it as such.

LIABILITY: It is the responsibility of the reader to exercise caution and discretion in all financial transactions, investments and planning. Both the publisher and author disclaim all warranties as to the appropriateness of all strategies, tactics and advice contained in this book to any specific situation, purpose or entity, either personal or commercial.

HYPERLINKS: Neither the publisher nor the author in any way endorse the information available at any hyperlinked websites, nor does any hyperlink imply an association with any hyperlinked websites, nor do the publisher or the author in any way vouch that the content remains what it was when first including the hyperlink in the book.

ENTITIES MENTIONED: Neither the publisher nor the author make any guarantees concerning any entity mentioned in this book, either personal or commercial, or in any way endorse any entity mentioned in this book, either personal or commercial, nor do they imply any association with any entity mentioned in this book, either personal or commercial.

FORMAT: This book is published in a variety of formats. The content published in one format might not be identical to the content published in another format. Furthermore, the content might be revised with subsequent editions or printings. Neither the publisher nor the author make any warranties that this copy is the most up-to-date or the most complete or the definitive edition or format at the time you are reading it.

ISBN: 978-0-9949115-0-6 (hardback)
ISBN: 978-0-9949115-1-3 (paperback)
ISBN: 978-0-9949115-2-0 (ebook)

Library & Archives Canada 2016 Victor Chiu.

Cover design by Miladinka Milic.
Photography by Patrick Chiu.
Illustrations by Ebimayo Studios.
Book design by Wordzworth.com
Editorial assistance provided by David Leonhardt of THGM.

Follow us on Twitter @moneyliveshere
Like us @ www.facebook.com/moneyliveshere
www.wallstreetkitchen.com
www.cherryisred.com

Mom,

When I said I wasn't going to talk about you in the book, I lied.

Love,
Victor

CONTENTS

Author's Preface		ix
Introduction		1
Chapter 1	Taking Stock	11
Chapter 2	Your Best Broker	31
Chapter 3	Why Trading Sucks	57
Chapter 4	The Profitable Art of Discipline	73
Chapter 5	Universal Truths	95
Chapter 6	Survival Tools	115
Chapter 7	The Media Is Your Enemy	143
Chapter 8	Mom's Ten Commandments of Investing	159
Chapter 9	An Hour in the Life of Mom	173
Chapter 10	The Recipe	191
Conclusion: You Get Rich		205
Mom's Recipes		209
Appendix		225
Index		229

AUTHOR'S PREFACE

Hello there!

Come in, come in. I'm so glad that you accepted my invitation. Mom's in the kitchen, let's join her there, follow me.

Obviously you're here to learn about Mom's secret recipe to investing – how to become wealthy even without much money to start with, just like her. Well, you won't be disappointed.

Take a look around our kitchen. On one side of the counter we prepare food. On the other side, we eat and invest. The cupboards are oak, not mahogany. The countertops laminate, not marble. Mom could afford to upgrade but that's not her style. She is a simple, sensible woman. And this is a simple, sensible kitchen. It's neither shabby nor ostentatious. This set-up works for us.

Have a seat. I hope you don't mind just chatting around our oak kitchen table. We're a modest family and quite frankly this is where all the action takes place. This is where Mom became independently wealthy.

You look surprised. Did you expect a fancy office with several computers and charts on the walls? No, Mom just sits at the kitchen table with her laptop, a Dell XPS M1530, which I gave her initially for the purpose of watching Korean dramas. That's all she does, that's all it takes. She concentrates yet she's pretty relaxed about it. And if you use Mom's recipe, you too can conquer Wall Street in your kitchen.

Do you know the best part? It's not that her approach is simple. The best part is that you can do it in the comfort of your own home – away from the frenzy of the trading floor on Wall Street.

Don't be fooled however, simple does not mean easy. However, if you stick to her disciplined approach and make decisions based on facts rather than on emotions, the stock market is the easiest way to build a great amount of wealth in a short amount of time. So, have a sip of our fragrant Oolong tea as I explain not just how but why we must all participate in the market.

Relax and enjoy the process as you become a super kitchen investor by gaining the knowledge and common sense to see the market through Mom's eyes. You will also pick up some of our guaranteed delicious, easy to cook, traditional family recipes along the way.

For those of you who have a knack for discovery, know that there is one hidden message contained in this book. The hidden message reveals Mom's character trait that is responsible for her stock market success. This trait is within all of us. The clues are scattered throughout every chapter so keep your eyes peeled and ears to the ground as you read. And no, I won't just blurt it out because the effect will be so much more powerful if you discover it on your own. But I will leave you with this clue: approach this book with a clear mind – dispose of everything you know about the stock market as what you already believe will make this hidden message more difficult to discover. If you approach this book with a blank canvas, the message will jump out at you by your final visit.

But if you came here expecting some miraculous ingredient, a secret sauce, an elixir or a magic potion to investing, I am afraid we don't have any of those.

No gimmicks. No hocus pocus. Just a recipe (and a hidden message) that can make you a lot of money.

INTRODUCTION

"If you really want to make a friend, go to someone's house and eat with him ... the people who give you their food give you their heart."

—Cesar Chavez

This is Mom; Mom, this is our new reader. I am Mom's son, Victor Chiu. Mom doesn't talk much, but I am sure she will correct me or jump in if I miss anything important. For me, she is a strong, powerful force as she stands there. She doesn't have to say much to have a big impact on everybody around her.

> *Oh, Victor. You flatter me. "Strong" is probably not the best word for me. I have a bad lower back and my knee never recovered from surgery many years ago. But you don't have to be physically strong to get wealthy.*

Well, Mom, you are strong in my eyes. And our reader will see why soon enough.

I'm glad you're making yourself feel at home now. First, I assume you want some background. After all, you should not take financial advice from just anybody. It's always best to take advice from somebody who has actually done it, and Mom has – which makes her the expert. Oh, Mom, don't blush; we are all so proud of how your common sense and discipline made you wealthy.

Our story starts when we arrived in Canada. We came from Hong Kong in 1989. That's not all that long ago, but I was just five years old at the time. Mom, Dad, Big Brother, Little Sister and I settled in Vancouver. Mom and Dad sold our apartment in Hong Kong, and that gave them just enough to buy a house, appliances, furniture and a Pontiac Sunbird. Not quite rags, but the designer names we were wearing were certainly not Gucci or Armani; they were more like Levi's and American Eagle.

This is not a "rags to riches" story. It was more like a Levi's to the whatever-we-choose-to-wear story, except we now choose to wear Levi's because we like to. When you're wealthy and don't have to clock eight hours a day in an office, you get the choice.

You know, it's funny to see the faces of our friends when they ask my sister and me, "Where do your parents work?", and we tell them, "They don't. Mom cooks and shops, and Dad golfs and watches TV all day."

But our "Levi's to riches" story isn't that simple. It was a huge risk moving to Canada, because Dad had to leave behind his business connections, and his skill sets in textiles were simply not in demand here in Canada.

Before making it, we had to live small. Very small. My grandmother had joined us, so we were six in the house with no steady income. Fortunately, Mom is much disciplined, so we lived frugally and spent very little. That discipline made her a stock market success. It's that same discipline that Mom and I will teach you around this kitchen table.

> *Victor, our guest might want to know what I accomplished. I mean, why should anybody listen to a simple housewife like me, if they don't know exactly how successful my approach has proven itself to be?*

Mom's right. Before I spill the beans on exactly what to do, I'll bet you're curious to know just how well Mom did. How about a cup of Oolong tea while we go over a bit of history?

Thanks, Mom. That's good tea.

Just to put things in perspective, you recall how I said we arrived in Canada in 1989? That was with enough money to buy a middle-class lifestyle, with some corner-cutting, but we struggled with income after that. Mom was buying fruits and vegetables in season and on special. We made do without a lot of things for a while.

I was not telling the kids in grade school that Mom cooks and shops, and that Dad golfs and watches TV all day long. It was not until 2006 that Mom launched her stock market investing program. By then, she had saved up $40,000.

That was her initial investment – $40,000. It could have been lower. She could have begun investing earlier. But that's where she started. You could start earlier if you wish. You can buy any number of shares, but most typically people are offering their shares for sale in batches of 100 at a time. If a company's shares are selling for $28, you will most likely need at least $2,800 to begin with, although you might find someone selling just 50 shares or 25. I have bought 25 shares before, but it is not the most common number available.

Yes, you could buy stock from companies with much lower share values, often called "penny stocks", but then Mom might have to put an extra tablespoon of cayenne pepper in your tea, just to teach you a lesson, right Mom? I am kidding, of course, but seriously – don't buy penny stocks. Mom and I will go over that with you later.

Mom, you can put back the cayenne pepper, now.

Mom's goal was – and still is – to own as many quality stocks as possible within her lifetime by following a simple, practical process that she replicates over and over.

Mom's first $40,000 investment bought her shares in TD Bank, Royal Bank and ScotiaBank. Yes, three banks; you are sharp to notice that. I will explain later why she invested in banks. But for now, let me tell you that she made $25,000 of profit from those banks.

I should mention that she also bought some other stocks in those early years. Perhaps you recognize names like Guang Zhou Global Telecom Inc. (GZGT), China VOIP & Digital (CVDT) and Mabcure Inc. (MBCI)? No? Don't you recognize them? Here's the laptop – go ahead, look them up.

OK, I'll tell you why you can't find them. Either nobody trades the stock anymore or they no longer exist, that's why. These were "over the counter" penny stocks, highly speculative, and they lost all their value.

An interesting note is how Mom was sold on the GZGT stock back in 2007. This was part of their sales pitch: "Our last stock pick from China, CVDT, shot up an incredible 154% …" So was this: "As professionals always on the lookout for growth opportunities within emerging markets, we are excited to ..."

It turns out that marketing is just marketing and, well, we should know better than to even listen to marketing.

Mom also bought some less speculative stocks, like Bombardier and Rediff, but I mention these just in passing.

During 2007 and 2008, she invested her profit in three other companies: Enbridge, Pembina, and Suncor Energy. Yes, three energy companies – you are sharp again. But more important than these companies being energy companies is that they pay a typical dividend of 3 to 5 percent.

If you are a student of recent history, you will recall what happened in October of 2008. That's right, stock markets around the world collapsed and the media was filled with doom and gloom and shades of 1929.

Mom did not panic. She did cut her losses, so to speak, by selling off the few small- to mid-sized companies she held. Those penny stocks? Gone. Bombardier and Rediff? Gone. She held firm on the other ones, right Mom?

> *That's right. You know, I've seen enough stock market crashes in my lifetime, both in North America and in Asia. I wasn't worried. I knew that any drop this severe could only be temporary. It was just a matter of time before the market was bound to rebound and rise from the ashes. It had to happen.*

Exactly. So Mom held tight onto her blue chip stocks – the "Mom Stocks". What happened next is exciting. The economy picked up in 2009, just as Mom knew it would. That's why she's wearing that smug smile.

So Mom took the money she got from the sale of the small- and mid-sized company stocks, as well as the dividends from the stocks she held on to and invested them in Magna International and AutoCanada. She also bought shares in Canadian Pacific Railway and Brookfield Infrastructure Partners. Once again, you are sharp to notice that we are looking at companies related to transportation and logistics.

Over the course of 2010 – 2011, Mom invested the profits from AutoCanada, Magna International, Canadian Pacific Railway and Brookfield infrastructure in insurance stocks, specifically Manulife, Sun Life, and MetLife. When I say "profits", I mean the dividends that she earned from those companies, as well as the sale of shares representing her original investment in each stock. She does not sell off the growth because that's the "house money" she plays with. So she keeps reinvesting the same money over and over, plus the dividends while the profits from each stock continue to grow.

During 2011-2012, the pattern continues. Mom took the profits she earned from Manulife, Sun Life, and MetLife and her older holdings, and invested them in Bristol-Myers Squibb and Merck & Co. So now she's into pharmaceuticals, as well as all the other sectors of the economy that she had previously bought into.

So that's her six-year, 1000% run. All her dividends were reinvested in the market, with the exception of some of the dividends from her energy and bank stocks, which she occasionally used to provide for the family. All her gains stayed where they were, to keep creating profits. And all the original investments in various stocks were pulled out to invest in new stocks.

As I'm sitting here writing this in 2015, her portfolio grew from the 3 bank stocks to 46 stocks today as she continues to use her same recipe she started with back in 2006.

I know what you want to ask. Didn't everybody make money from the lows of 2009 to the highs of 2012?

Well, if you look at the North American market as a whole during Mom's investing period, the Dow Jones index hit a bottom of 7062.93 points in 2009 which rebounded to a high of 13437.13 points in 2012. The New York Stock Exchange's lowest was 5195.79 in 2009 and recovered to the highest 2012 point at 8443.51. The Toronto Stock index, between 7591.50 and 14252.80 in the same period. This meant if you invested on any of these indices you would have roughly doubled your original investment in 3 years. Mom's method made 10 times that of her original investment, that's 5 times more than the average market return!

You may also tell me if you bought into a random single stock during that time, say, XYZ stock, you could have made 15 or 20 times more in the same period from 2009 and 2012. And it's true, I believe it! Some stocks did go on a tear but to have picked the right stock would have had more to do with luck than anything else, and that is not what this book is about. We all want luck, but we don't want to rely on it.

You may also think all this sounds too easy, or at least too simple. You want to know what her system was to decide what to buy, when to sell, how to choose stocks, how to time them, how to value companies and what's the best way to monitor progress and watch for early warning signs.

I don't promise that we will cover everything you want to know in great detail in our little kitchen table chats. I will not tell you everything you will ever want to know, and you should not assume that everything I tell you is everything you need to know. In fact, you should never rely on just one source of information. Life is about learning, and a serious investor should never stop learning about investing.

But I do promise to discuss why she chose those stocks because it will give you an important pattern you can adopt for your own investments.

While to some degree solid investment decisions can be made through rigorous mathematical analysis of available data, we will not be getting into that. Mom and I believe that solid investment decisions can also be made through the investment philosophy we are sharing with you here.

I can't prove to you that Mom's cooking tastes the best, and I won't try. In the same way, I do not and will not provide a rigorous mathematical proof for the effectiveness of our philosophy. I firmly believe mathematical proofs and transaction details will be counterproductive to helping you grasp what we will be sharing with you.

I have watched Mom invest over the course of many years, and I am going to share Mom's recipe for wealth. Nothing I say, nothing she says, nothing we discuss should be a substitute for learning how to read charts or make sense of data. This kitchen is the place to learn the basics, the foundation for investing.

And nothing we tell you implies that other strategies don't work. There are so many ways to prepare wontons – did you know that you can make a delicious meal by frying wontons instead of boiling them in broth? And there are so many ways to get rich from the stock market.

So make a point of discovering other strategies and techniques found elsewhere, too. What I am sharing is Mom's recipe for investing. I can also share her wonton recipes with you[1] if you are interested, but my invitation that brought you here is to learn about how she invests. I've deconstructed and simplified her recipe down to what I think is the essence of her success – the key ingredients, the utensils she uses and the approach she takes to combining the ingredients.

I'll give you a sneak peek at her formula. It's a theory, but it's the base for everything we'll talk about.

---

[1] All recipes mentioned in this book are genuine Mom recipes that can be found at the end of the book.

1. Buy Stock A.
2. Stock A price rises > sell some Stock A
3. Use Stock A proceeds to buy Stock B
4. Stock B rises > sell some Stock B
5. Use proceeds to buy stock C
6. Stock C rises > sell some Stock C

See? Pretty simple. But putting it into practice does require understanding a few good principles.

There are countless books out there teaching you how to perform complex calculations and analyses. If you wish to read a great book on analysis, I recommend *The Intelligent Investor* by Benjamin Graham. There are countless guides on data crunching and how to use advanced mathematical techniques to profit from the market. And there are countless financial gurus happy to lead you through algorithms and charts, and how to predict minute-by-minute movements of stock and futures and commodities.

You'll find none of that around Mom's kitchen table. I don't have any math or algorithms or insider secrets to share with you, just battle-tested practical knowledge and wisdom that you can apply today. We will be sharing the philosophy behind the success of a typical stay-at-home housewife. It could be anybody, but Mom is a stay-at-home housewife with no formal education in the field of finances. If she can do it – and she did! – so can you.

These are timeless teachings. Your grandchildren will be able to use them. You can take them to London or Tokyo or New York City – wherever there are stable markets. We'll help fine-tune your brain so that you can apply her thought process and her approach to whatever investing you choose to do.

Mom taught me everything I know, and it took me five years for me to learn. I watched. I asked questions. And together, we'll show you how she did it.

She taught me to be an investor, not a trader, and I'll show you how. She taught me how to escape the self-sabotaging emotions that sink many people like you and me, and I'll show you how. She taught me how to plan for success, and I'll show you how. She taught me how to stick to the plan, and I'll show you how. She taught me how to separate facts form opinion, and I'll show you how. She taught me how to play the long game, and I'll show you how. She taught me how to win, and I'll show you how.

And it won't take you five years because all our kitchen table chats are condensed into one, simple book.

No, you won't learn everything from Mom. But you will walk away from here with a sound investing philosophy that can underpin any strategy or technique you learn somewhere else.

The next time you come, we'll sit around this table again, and we'll start talking a bit about the stock market and how we see it. This is crucial to understand if you want to learn to play it the way we do. But don't worry, we'll be just as relaxed then as we are now.

Mom's an amazing person, a simple stay-at-home mother with no more than high school education raising three kids and feeding a family of six while making a fortune in the stock market. I just don't know how she did it. Well, actually, I do know at least the stock market part. You'll have to go elsewhere for advice on raising kids.

CHAPTER 1
Taking Stock

*"Give a man a fish and you feed him for a day.
Teach a man to fish, and you feed him for lifetime."*

—Chinese Proverb/Anonymous

Welcome back.

Come on in. You know where the kitchen table is, just before the beige island counter, so please just head straight in and have a seat. We have something very exciting cooked up for you today.

In fact, today we are going to look at why it is so profitable to invest in the stock market, and …

Ah, I see you are wondering what that savoury-smelling dish is in front of you? Mom cooked something up, just for you (well, also for me – I don't want you to have all the fun!). Remember on your last visit, I told you that we can make a delicious meal by frying wontons instead of boiling them in broth? Well, Mom made up a batch of her world-famous Crispy Pan Fried Wontons with wasabi mayo dipping sauce.

Go ahead ... taste it.

Mmmm-mmmm. Pretty good, eh? I can feel the flavour right down to my toes.

This is more than just a free meal. These wontons carry a very valuable financial lesson that we will explore today. Many people are raised on the notion that the best way to manage their money is to put it away in "savings". This often means bank deposits. Sometimes it means savings bonds. These savings are a lot like wonton soup; everybody knows them, but they are bland and don't really perk up your taste buds. It's more like parking your money than investing it.

Start thinking differently with your ingredients, and you get the taste sensation of Crispy Pan Fried Wontons. Right, mom?

> *Right. Start thinking differently with your finances, and you get the wealth sensation of the stock market.*
>
> *Your little snack won't last very long, and you'll be hungry again in a few hours. But the information Victor is about to share with you will last you a lifetime.*

Exactly. You see, there are many ways to invest that go beyond "savings". Some are riskier than others. Some require more knowledge than others. The stock market is neither risky nor requires particular knowledge when you follow Mom's recipe for stock market investing.

Mom, what's with the Mona Lisa smile?

> *Nothing. Just please continue. You're doing just fine, Victor.*

I think that smile means that she likes what I'm saying. Mind you, I am not suggesting that real estate is a bad investment. Build a man a house, and he'll watch TV for decades. Teach a man to build a house, and the renovations will never end. Real estate takes upkeep.

Nor that commodities and precious metals and other investments are without merit. But do you understand the differences between pork bellies and cotton futures? It's not all that obvious, and frankly, I've never felt like asking Mom to cook up a pot of pork bellies.

It's the method and the discipline that will keep you from wanton spending on useless or low value investments.

What's so special about the stock market? It's certainly not like the market where Mom gets all her fresh fruits and vegetables. What Mom buys at the stock market sits on this kitchen table for years, right in this laptop. It doesn't rot. It doesn't smell. It just grows wealth.

What Mom buys at the local market would rot if you leave them to sit on this kitchen table. They would grow mould instead of wealth, and they would probably put you off your Crispy Pan Fried Wontons. And if you tried putting them on the laptop – no, I don't even want to think about it.

What do the two markets have in common? They both provide for Mom's family. The local market provides fruits and veggies and meats and all sorts of great stuff to eat. The stock market provides the money to buy whatever we want at the local market. So you could say that stock market money tastes good.

While you are finishing up your snack, let's look at the reasons to invest in the stock market. Don't ask yourself if you can afford to invest, rather ask yourself can you afford NOT to?!

FIRST, so that your hard-earned money can work for YOU

This is somewhat of a counterintuitive way of thinking. Most people are raised to believe that they have to work for their money, like money's the boss and they are the slaves. Money cracks the whip.

Row faster! >CRACK!<

Dig deeper! >CRACK!<

Pound harder! >CRACK!<

With the stock market, YOU crack the whip. (CAUTION: Please do not take this literally. Cracking an actual whip in any stock market is likely to earn you a mug shot.) But with stocks, you ARE the boss and you ARE in control and your money DOES work for you.

Mom invests in stocks because it allows her to have the freedom to take care of her family and her home at her leisure. Yes, the key word is leisure. She does not have to row or dig or pound or ask "Would you like fries with that?" to provide for her family.

> *But sometimes I do serve fries. That's the beauty of it. I can serve my family whatever I choose.*

Being able to eat whatever we like is leisure, too. Have I overstated things with the word "leisure"? Being a housewife is a full-time job. It's not like Mom lounges around all day. But she can be a housewife at a leisurely pace, rather than frantically trying to balance and juggle everything like a crazed busker on the street corner. She saw that the stock market could effectively provide for her family without having to trade hours for dollars.

In other words, she could earn money while going grocery shopping. You can't do that while rowing.

She could earn money while preparing all our breakfasts, lunches, and dinners day in and day out. You can't do that while digging.

She could earn money while cleaning up our messes. You can't do that while pounding.

Mom doesn't work for her money; Mom's money works for her.

> *When Victor was young, I introduced him to the concept of other people paying me money without me having to working for it.*

Stop and think about it for a moment. People pay you money, and you don't have to do any work. Is that crazy, or what? The idea just blew my mind. I thought that was the coolest thing ever. I still do.

Wouldn't you love to have somebody just walk up to you and hand you free money? You bet!

But this is counter intuitive for most people. In fact, most people actually refuse free money when it is handed to them. Every year, Alex Feldman tries to give away free Money on the streets of Boston, and every year people have the same reaction: "What's the catch?"

People dream of free money. They will invent elaborate schemes to make more money, doing less work. They'll buy into MLM schemes (multi-level marketing), selling antifungal shampoos and patches that ward of the heebeejeebees. They'll take huge risks and pay large amounts to get free money. But they won't take free money if somebody offers it.

So I am asking you, will you take it? Mom and I have a method for getting people to give you free money. You take the money, and you do not have to work for it. Are you willing to put aside your natural suspicion – your emotions – and follow us into the stock market armed only with the facts, and make money without working for it?

You are willing? Good.

Because this really is the coolest thing ever. This is the simple notion of setting up a system just once, and that system will run itself and pay you for a lifetime with little to no effort on your part. It's almost completely "set it, and forget it". And I'm not selling you any program you need to buy into with a secret handshake and a monthly order of antifungal shampoos.

Here, let me show you real quick by sketching out the concept on this napkin:

Hey, my drawing isn't too bad, no? I spoke of leisure earlier, and of course being a housewife isn't leisure, but here's the really exciting part. The stock market earns you money while you eat, while you sleep, while you pet your dog and while you try to break the world record for the most blueberry pies consumed in a single sitting. So you do get paid for your leisure time, too, whatever your leisure may be.

You get paid to eat a slice of blueberry pie; you get paid to eat twenty blueberry pies. It doesn't matter. Whatever you do for leisure, you get paid to do it. The only difference is that you'll have more of a mess to clean up after 20 blueberry pies, and you might need to rush to the hospital. But the really good news is that you will still get paid while in the hospital.

To get financially ahead, you need your money to work for you, not the other way around. That's the secret of the rich. And that's the secret that has allowed Mom to spend the time making Crispy Pan Fried Wontons for us today.

While Mom's tidying up the dishes – Thanks, Mom. That was delicious – let's look at a few more reasons to invest in the stock market.

SECOND, the stock market pulverizes inflation

We touched earlier on savings, but we didn't really talk about them. If you want something totally risk-free, why not just put your money in the bank? Because of inflation. Inflation is an exciting little piece of magic that allows you to lose money with no effort on your part. You don't have to gamble. You even don't have to hand out free money on street corners. You just have to put the money in the bank and – POOF! – like magic, it will shrink year after year. Unless your bank account pays a lot more in interest than inflation takes away, putting money in the bank is a great way to become unwealthy.

For most of the 1990s and 2000s, inflation has been low, around 2 percent. But that has not always been the case, and people forget that inflation could get very high once again. For most of the 1980s, inflation was around 4-5 percent. And for most of the 1970s inflation was over eight percent, peaking at above 12 percent in 1981. Imagine 10 years of inflation at over five percent. Your money could shrink so much that you'll need to bring a microscope with you to the bank.

What about putting your money into something secure that pays a guaranteed interest rate? Surely that will beat inflation, right?

Wrong!

In 2012, Canadian tax expert Evelyn Jacks calculated the real after-tax profits a person would make on a ten-year $1000 "investment" in Canada Savings Bonds. She added the interest, subtracted the tax, and adjusted for inflation, and PRESTO!

Her $1000 had grown to $855.90 in just ten years.

I'll let you turn that one over in your mind for a moment while I help Mom with the tea.

So you see, inflation is like rot. It gets into all your money and eats it up. You can't just put money aside and hope that it will twiddle its thumbs year after year and still be there waiting for you like a faithful dog after all that time.[2]

You need the money to work for you. If your money gets to sit around leisurely all day long, you will have to work for it. If your money works for you, you get to sit around leisurely all day long.

It's very simple – the work has to get done, so it's either you or your money that will have to do the rowing, the digging, and the pounding. Which will it be?

THIRD, you don't have to trade hours for dollars

For the working class (that's most people when you think about it), there is a limit to how much a person can make. There are only 24 hours per day, and chances are that you won't want to spend more than 23 of them working. Many people work even less. This is a very fair system, by the way. Each of us has the same number of hours to work, so if we each trade our hours for money, we can each earn the same amount of money. We can choose to trade as many or as few hours as we wish for dollars.

But we can't have both. The more hours we want for doing things other than work, the less money we will have. And the more money we want for buying things we need or like, the less time we will have to enjoy those things.

With a job, as soon as you stop working, you stop earning. Want to cook a meal? You stop earning. Want to fix your car? You stop

---

[2] People will continue to combat inflation by investing their money into investment vehicles like real estate, bonds, and stocks. No wonder there is no stopping the market's climb – over 100 years and counting!

earning. Want to watch YouTube video fail compilations all day? You don't earn any money from a job while watching videos, not even fail compilations. Want to eat twenty blueberry pies and spend the next two days in the hospital? You stop earning.

And after paying the bills, after buying clothing and groceries, after tallying up all the expenses, you discover what "job" actually stands for: Just Over Broke.

If you don't have to work for your money, if somebody hands you money for free, you get to keep both your time and your money. As I said earlier, the idea just blew my mind. But it is counterintuitive for most people, so most people just get a job and trade their time – their life! – for money. That's not really living, is it?

Want to know what's even worse? You're getting older. I know, it's not fair, but it is true. You and I are getting older. Even Mom is getting older. There will come a time when working will get harder.

Rowing will get harder.

Digging will get harder.

Pounding will get harder.

But accepting free money from the stock market won't get harder.

There will come a time when we will have to stop working. But we can still accept free money from the stock market at any age. The stock market is like golf: start anytime, play at any age.

There might come a time when you will be replaced by somebody else, or even by a machine (pretty sad to think of, eh?) So we won't be able to rely on jobs or even pensions to retire on.

By the way, pensions are not all that great. They usually require us to downscale our lifestyles. Would it not be better to be able to retire earlier with more money? Then who cares about the machines that replace us? Let them work for their money, while our money works for us.

FOURTH, you get an unfair advantage

The stock market is like a machine that prints money. Of course, the stock market is not that simple, but you earning money from the stock market is that simple. Is this fair?

Of course not. Fair is when everybody works the same number of hours and earns the same amount of money and struggles with the same amount of expenses and pulls their hair out from the same amount of stress.

Fair sucks.

The stock market is unfair. Knowing how to make the stock market work for you gives you an unfair advantage. In fact, right now, this very minute, thousands of people are making money while they sleep, eat and crochet Christmas tree decorations for their grandchildren. There is, at least, one lady I know who is making money from the stock market while she prepares Crispy Pan Fried Wontons. They have an unfair advantage over you. Mom has an unfair advantage over you.

The stock market is unfair, and if you earn your money working, you are the sucker in the equation. Sorry to be so blunt, but that's the fact. If you have a job, you are the person handing the stock market investors their free money. You are working for your money, and your money is working for them. That is the concept of the stock market. That is how it works.

The good news is that the stock market is equally unfair to everybody. As Ryan T. O'Donnell, CFO at The O'Donnell Group in Chico, California says, "It is highly regulated, meaning Joe Schmo can have as good an opportunity as Donald Trump."

No, it's not fair. But life isn't fair. Things turn out to your advantage or to your detriment, and often it is based on the choices you make.

Will you choose the stock market, or will you pass it by? If you pass it by, that will be the second biggest mistake you could make. Whether you choose to invest wisely in the stock market or pass it by, it will continue to move money from some people toward other people. It will continue to be unfair. It's just a matter of whether you will benefit from it or suffer from it.

What's that? You want to know what would be the biggest mistake you could make? Passing on Mom's Crispy Pan Fried Wontons. They are really good, aren't they?

FIFTH, inclusivity

Anybody can enter the stock market. You don't have to live in the right neighborhood or wear the right clothes. There is no substance use testing. You don't need to have security clearance or a name tag. And you don't need a specific amount of money.

If you want to buy real estate, you need a lot of money to start with. Real estate comes in large increments. The stock market is easy to enter, and that is one reason Mom took an early interest in it, right Mom?

Don't you love Mom's smile?

You can enter the stock market with $1000 or $10 million. You can enter at any point in between. The only caveat if you plan to enter at the lower end is that you might find it hard to find stocks for sale in batches of fewer than 100 at a time, so you might need to exercise a little extra patience. And you want to avoid buying stocks that are too cheap. We'll get to that at a later session, but for now, just remember what I mentioned last time about how Mom might have to put an extra tablespoon of cayenne pepper in your tea to teach you a lesson if you start buying "penny stocks".

SIXTH, liquidity

Do you know what "liquidity" means? Something that is liquid is easy to pour. When Mom makes a delicious Italian sauce, she might make it more liquid for certain dishes and more chunky for others. The one with more liquidity is easy to pour; just tip the pot and it all flows out. The chunky one won't flow as easily, and you need a spatula to scrape it all out of the pan.

Investments are like that, too. Some are easier to sell than others. This is critical if an emergency happens and you need to free up some money quickly. Stocks are liquid for two reasons.

First, stocks are easy to sell. You put them up for sale and within 24 to 48 hours you have the money. There is always someone interested in buying your stocks, although you might have to be a little flexible in price. Still, you will get fair market price on the day you sell, even if you had been planning to hold on to them longer and sell them for more.

Have you ever tried to sell a property or a business overnight? You won't get your money in 24 hours. Nor in a week. Most likely not in a month. And there you are trying to handle an emergency, desperately needing to free up some money, and having to waste time fiddling with a myriad of details that the sale of a house or business entails – documentation, property inspections, meeting with agents and buyers, negotiations, etc. Stocks sell much faster, and with little or no effort.

Second, stocks can be sold in part. If you own 500 shares of a company, you can easily sell off 100 or 300 shares, depending on how much cash you need to free up. You can't do that with real estate or with a business. It's all or nothing. Even if you can and know how to slice your land or business and sell it in part, it will take you much longer than 48 hours.

Stocks sell:
- Quickly.
- Easily.
- In convenient proportions.

SEVENTH, scalability

Stocks are scalable, which means that you can buy or sell them in whatever quantity you wish. As I just mentioned, you can start out with $1000 or $10 million, whatever you have available. For buying, they are completely scalable.

As I also just mentioned, you can sell 100 shares or 300 shares, or you could sell 10,000 shares. In fact, you can sell as many as you own, and you can even sell more than you own through a clever sleight-of-hand called "short selling" (which takes things to a higher level of risk and expertise that I don't think would be Mom-approved). So for selling, stocks are completely scalable.

It goes without saying that the revenue you earn form stocks is scalable, as well. How much you earn is directly proportional to how much you invest. If you invest $1000, and the return is 5%, you will earn $50. That's not a lot, but you didn't invest a lot. If you invest a million dollars, your return would be $50,000. That's a lot, but don't forget that you invested a lot. What's important in scalability isn't to look at the actual dollar amount of return, but rather the percentage of return.

The exciting thing is that even if you invested only $1000, you can then invest another $1000 when you have the money to do so. And another. And another. Because the increments required to invest are relatively small, stocks are scalable over time, as well.

You don't have to eat twenty blueberry pies all at once, but you can still eat twenty blueberry pies. One slice at a time. As much as you are actually hungry for. No hospital visit necessary. Eat at your own pace. Invest at your own pace.

EIGHTH, stocks are simply the best long-term investment, period

When you own stock, you own a piece of a company. That's what a stock is. You own a piece of the management, including the president, the product developers, the marketing team, the patent lawyers and the executives. You own a piece of the company mascot and the branding strategy. You own a piece of the ingenuity and creativity, a piece of the intellectual force behind the company. And, of course, you own a piece of the profits.

Do big companies make profit?

If you own a share of the company, you own a share of the profits. Want to know the crazy thing about the president, the patent lawyers, the executives and even the mascot? They are all working for you. Everything they do is geared toward sending you free money. They are like a printing press. They are a machine churning out money for you.

They do this while you sleep. They do this while you eat. They do this while you try to think up an excuse to be far away when the in-laws come over for dinner. This is why stocks are the best investment overall, and all you have to do is buy them.

Do you know what *CNN* has to say about stock performances: "Stocks have historically provided the highest returns of any asset class – close to 10% over the long term [past 100 years]. The next best performing asset class is bonds. Long-term U.S. Treasuries have returned an average of more than 5%."

You might have heard some people talk about property values and that real estate is the best long-term investment. Both real estate and

Owning Stocks = Owning Companies

stocks have a good record, they both occasionally crash, and they both bounce back time after time. So which one is better?

Rob Carrick investigated this in *The Globe and Mail*, and found that from 2004 to 2013, real estate appreciated 5.4% annually, whereas stocks appreciated just under 8%. Looking at it from 1994 through 2013, real estate appreciated by 5.5% per year, and stocks appreciated by 8.5%.

In other words, stocks beat out bonds and real estate by significant margins. For long-term wealth creation, stocks are the best performers.

I'm not trying to discourage you from investing in real estate at any point. But from my experience stocks are a lot less of a headache and require a lot less money to get started than real estate. In fact, the very reason I got into stocks is so that I could eventually purchase property! But I fell in love with stocks on the journey there. And I bet you will too.

Dow Jones Industrial Average History of Values

The Dow, as financial groupies affectionately call it, is the oldest general financial stock index in the United States. It measures the value of the 30 most significant publicly traded stocks. Because of the sheer size and influence these 30 stocks have on the market, most experts say the Dow dictates the movement of all other US stock exchanges! So it is fair to say that, at least for our purpose, we can use the Dow index to represent the US stock market as a whole.

I know this is just a simple chat around the kitchen table, and I promise not to pull out dozens of charts and graphs and mathematical equations that would bamboozle even Mr. Peabody. But I will bring out just a few to help you see what's going on. So take a look at these 2 graphs on the laptop:

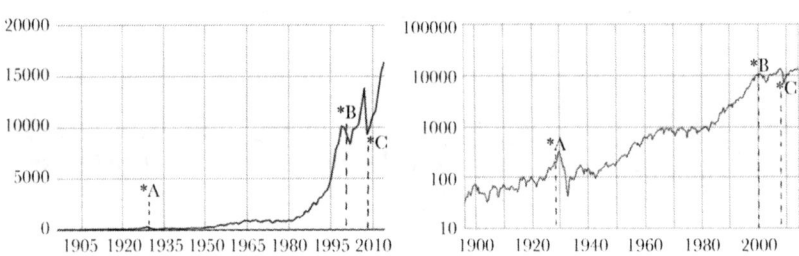

Dow Jones Industrial Average from 1896 to 2014

*A – Crash in 1929
*B – Dot Com crash in 2000
*C – Financial crisis in 2008

The left is a linear chart of the Dow Jones Industrial Average from 1896 to 2014 and the right is an identical graph but a scaled version of it. I plotted 3 disasters: the infamous 1929 Great Crash, and 2 in recent memory: the 2000 Dot Com Crash and 2008 Financial Crisis. The left hand chart plots the 3 disasters as the Dow continues its accelerated upward trajectory. The right hand chart reveals even through the countless hardship the world faced in the last 100 and some years these events register only as minor blips on the index.

The point is, you can see just how resilient the market is. Even after the Great Crash of 1929, stocks dipped only for a few years, then returned to normal. People who bought at the height of the pre-depression bubble had to wait 25 years to recover their losses, but anyone who had been investing with a long-term view recovered much earlier.

What Mom and I find exciting about the Dow, is that there is not a name in the Index that the average Joe on the street won't recognize. Microsoft. Nike. Coca-Cola. DuPont. Chevron. Visa. Walmart. Proctor & Gamble. All the usual suspects and celebrity brands are gathered in one place and tracked year over year.

Even during the Great Depression (1929-1939), people wise enough to hold on to their stocks were making income from the dividends. Wharton finance professor Jeremy Siegel analyzed the effects of the Great Depression and found that the inflation-adjusted total return index of the U.S. stock market returned to its precrash peak by 1936-37, less than eight years after the crash[3]. And let's not forget that the pre-crash level was an unnaturally high spike to compare things to.

For a true picture of the historical rate of return from the stock market, you have to factor in the dividends. When you do, you see that even during the 1930s, the losses were minimal, and far, far less than the gains posted in the 1940s. Even with the crash of 2008, the stock market still performed acceptably across the 2000s and posted over 16% in returns from 2010 to 2013.

---

[3] Barron's Financial Investment News at *http://www.barrons.com/articles/ SB123637914471857307*

For those of you who love numbers, here is the history of returns to reveal how the Dow Index fared since 1901.[1]

Dow Jones Industrial Average Data Set from 1901 to 2014

Year	Percentage	Year	Percentage	Year	Percentage	Year	Percentage
1901	-8.7	1931	-52.7	1959	16.4	1987	2.3
1902	-0.4	1932	-23.1	1960	-9.3	1988	11.8
1903	-23.6	1933	66.8	1961	18.7	1989	27
1904	41.7	1934	4.1	1962	-10.8	1990	-4.3
1905	38.2	1935	38.6	1963	17	1991	20.3
1906	-1.9	1936	24.8	1964	14.6	1992	4.2
1907	-37.7	1937	-32.8	1965	10.9	1993	13.7
1908	46.6	1938	28	1966	-18.9	1994	2.1
1909	15	1939	-3	1967	15.2	1995	33.5
1910	-17.9	1940	-12.7	1968	4.3	1996	26
1911	0.4	1941	-15.3	1969	-15.2	1997	22.6
1912	7.6	1942	7.6	1970	4.8	1998	16.1
1913	-10.3	1943	13.8	1971	6.1	1999	25.2
1914	-30.7	1944	12.1	1972	14.6	*2000	-6.2
1915	81.7	1945	26.7	1973	-16.6	2001	-7.1
1917	-4.2	1946	-8.1	1974	-27.6	2002	-16.8
1918	10.5	1947	2.2	1975	38.3	2003	25.3
1919	30.5	1948	-2.1	1976	17.9	2004	3.1
1920	-32.9	1949	13.1	1977	-17.3	2005	-0.6
1921	12.7	1950	17.4	1978	-3.1	2006	16.3
1922	21.7	1951	14.4	1979	4.2	2007	6.4
1923	-3.3	1952	8.4	1980	14.9	*2008	-33.8
1924	26.6	1953	-3.8	1981	-9.2	2009	18.8
1925	30	1954	44	1982	19.6	2010	11
1926	0.3	1955	20.8	1983	20.3	2011	5.5
1927	28.8	1956	2.3	1984	-3.7	2012	7.3
1928	48.2	1957	-12.8	1985	27.7	2013	26.5
*1929	-17.2	1958	34	1986	22.6	2014	7.52
1930	-33.8						

* Crash in 1929
* Dot Com crash in 2000
* Financial crisis in 2008

---

[1] Data sets in this chapter from *http://www.forecast-chart.com*

Stanford economist John B. Shoven, PhD, calls the Dow a flawed index[5], precisely because it does not account for dividend payouts. In a paper published in 2000, he estimates that if dividend had been included in the Index, it would have reached 250,000 points by then, rather than just 10,000.

As Tom Weary, Chief Investment Officer of Lau Associates, LLC, in Greenville, Delaware, says, "The stock market is an instrument of capitalism, and capitalism is the creator of wealth. Because, over time, wealth will accumulate in the capital markets, which is why you want to participate in it."

NINTH, stocks are low-maintenance

Not only do stocks perform better than real estate, but they give you fewer headaches. Remember that you want your money to work for you, not the other way around. If you have to deal with tenants, utility fees, moving costs, maintenance charges, property taxes etc. that can create a job for you, eat away at your profits, or both.

Stocks are really low maintenance. Some people watch their stocks every day, trying to time their trades. In most cases, these "traders" lose money doing that. I'll explain more about that in a later discussion. For now, just understand that an investor is not a trader, and if you want more money and less stress, you don't want to fiddle with your stocks every day.

It's the low maintenance that allows us to enjoy a life of leisure. It's the low maintenance that allows us to sit here and chat with you. There are some things that money just can't buy, and time is one of those things. Stocks allow us to keep both our time and our money. It's just a little workaround to that pesky time-is-money equation you might hear from time to time.

---

[5] The full study can be seen at: *http://www-siepr.stanford.edu/papers/pdf/99-16.pdf*

When you invest in the stock market, time is not money. Time is simply time. No need to trade time for money.

Speaking of time, I think it's time to wrap up this chat. Mom and I have other things to do. But we'll be chatting again real soon. When you come back, we'll show you how you are the best person to manage your own investments. Yes, you! Not a broker – please! But we'll chat about that in detail when you return.

Before you go, I have some homework for you – just a little challenge. Start paying attention to the stock market. Pick a few big-name stocks to watch. Choose names you recognize. Check how much their stock was worth ten years ago, 20 years ago and 30 years ago. Then watch how they do over the next few days. That's all. Pretty easy homework, right?

Enjoy the rest of the day.

WHAT YOU LEARNED ON THIS VISIT

Make your money work for you, not the other way around.

Stocks rock – they beat inflation.

Don't trade hours for dollars.

You can have an unfair advantage.

The stock market always recovers if you stick with it.

Stocks are a low-maintenance investment.

CHAPTER 2
Your Best Broker

> *If you want a thing done well, do it yourself.*
>
> —Napoleon Bonaparte

Hello again.

Glad to see you could make it for another little kitchen table chat. Please come in.

You like the smell? Yes, I think you'll enjoy this. It's a favourite family recipe, but it's one that is so easy to do it yourself, right Mom?

> *It's easy to make. It's my ground beef spaghetti, with a little extra secret ingredient. Taste it. Ah, you like? Yes. The extra ingredient is fenugreek leaves. Gives it an exotic flavor. But the rest of the ingredients are your standard spaghetti sauce ingredients. Exactly what you would expect. I'll put a little bit in a Ziplock bag for you to take home with you.*

Thanks for making this Mom. It's not quite like the sauce you buy at the store. Some things are just better when you do them yourself.

If you recall, last time we talked about why stocks are such a great investment, compared to bonds and real estate and other possibilities. Remember I told you that one of the benefits is that stocks are more "liquid", just like a gravy? You can more easily sell them if you need to in a pinch. Whereas real estate or a business is less liquid, like a chunky sauce, and it takes a lot more time and effort to sell them.

This sauce is somewhat in between. And that is where you should be. Your investments should be liquid, but you should not be. That way, in a pinch, you can sell the stocks, but you should not sell them unless you absolutely have to.

Investments should be smooth.

You should be chunky. I mean that in a nice way, of course.

Which is why you should manage your own stock investments rather than hiring a broker, just as you would cook your own spaghetti sauce, rather than hiring someone to do it for you. You are wondering what liquidity has to do with who manages your stock portfolio? I shall get to that shortly.

But first I need to make it clear that doing it yourself is not the only effective way to run investments. If you want the help of a financial advisor, that's fine, just make sure it's a certified professional. There is a difference between financial advisors and brokers, which is important for you to understand.

The key difference is how a broker gets paid, which is transaction based. For instance, they earn a commission for each buy or sell order. Or each time you buy into a financial product, such as a mutual fund. In contrast, certified advisors have a fiduciary duty to act with undivided loyalty to you, the client. In other words, they occupy a position of special trust and confidence when working with clients.

Shall I share with you just some of the reasons that hiring a broker who makes his money on your transactions is just plain stupid?

FIRST, brokers don't have your interest at heart.

You see, you have your own interest at heart. Your sole reason to invest is to make money for yourself.

Your broker has his own interest at heart. His sole reason to help you is to make money for himself.

In theory, there is nothing wrong with that. Except for one minor detail. Your broker makes money only when you buy and sell, only when you trade. And that's where you lose. His genuine interest isn't to help your stocks make you money. His genuine interest is to persuade you to buy or sell as often as possible so that he makes commission on the trades.

When they sold Mom that GZGT stock in 2007, the "growth opportunity" turned out to be a loss opportunity. Marketing is just marketing, and they will say whatever they need to say to get you to buy. And sell. And buy again. In many cases, these are scams. In other cases, they are just aggressive marketing with no ill intent, but more often than not with ill effect.

Remember when I said last time that an investor is not a trader? Next time, we'll spend the whole session discussing why trading sucks. It really does. If you try trading, you'll lose big time. A broker has no interest in making you a successful investor because he does not make money from investors. He wants you to be a trader because he makes money from traders. And that really sucks.

You want your stocks to be liquid, sure. But you don't want to be pouring them out all the time. That is not in your interest. So you want to be chunky with your stocks, except when you absolutely need to sell.

By contrast, a certified financial planner should never be trying to convince you to buy or to sell against your own best interest. Their financial interest is in keeping you as a client, so they have to have your best interest at heart.

Are brokers scammers? I don't think most of them are, but they do exactly what you and I do. We do what is in our own self-interest to do. Oh, sure, we are all nice people. We help others out when we can. We smile. We are sociable. But when it comes time to make decisions, self-interest will always play a huge role. We can't help it; that is human nature. And since all the brokers I've ever met are human, they will act in their own self-interest.

So, you don't pay a broker to do what's in your own self-interest. You do pay him to do what is against your self-interest. Crazy, eh?

So why pay a broker at all?

Mom said to me at a young age, "Don't buy mutual funds or rely on brokers for your success in the market. We must invest for ourselves."

> *Victor, tell our friend that I never give my hard earned money away to brokers who sell commission-based mutual funds. Or actively managed mutual funds. We have all that information on index investing and dividend stock investing on this computer. We have it on the Internet. We do it ourselves. We pay fewer fees. We make more money.*

You heard it from Mom.

You notice that she mentions mutual funds. Mom doesn't like them. And a lot of personal finance groupies feel the same way. Mutual funds are a lot like brokers, only sneakier. They find a way to keep charging you, even when there is no need.

So let's go through the reasons why you don't need someone else to cook your spaghetti for you? Did I just say "spaghetti"? Well, it's not my fault. This sauce is just so good. But you also don't need somebody to handle your stock investments for you.

> *I made it myself, that's why it's so good. When I started out, I didn't hire a financial advisor. because I wanted to save money. But I found that managing these investments is easy, and even fun. So I just kept going.*

Exactly. You don't need a financial advisor because you can do it yourself. And I assume that if you are here, chatting with me, it is because you want to do it yourself, too.

But if you choose to hire a financial advisor, seek one who is required to put your needs before his. Look for one who does NOT combine product sales with advice-giving. Although some advisors do offer financial products, I recommend sticking strictly with a fee-only financial advisor. This is a pretty important point.

We have talked about whose interest the broker has at heart, and how he wants you to be a trader, not an investor. Here are a few more reasons to avoid brokers.

SECOND, brokers offer you exorbitant costs

Do you know why they're called "brokers"? It's because they are broker than you, where their sole objective is to charge you fees so that you do not profit.

There is a cost to buy and sell stocks. There is no way to avoid that since one way or the other somebody is handling the transaction. You can't just walk up to someone in the street and buy or sell stocks since you don't actually hold stocks in your hand. If anybody does walk up to you in the street trying to sell you stocks … run!

So you need to pay somebody to handle the transaction. That's fair. However, that does not mean you need to pay a full-service broker, nor take one's advice. In the 21st century, we have all sorts of discount brokerages and online resources for buying and selling stocks, and those do not come with unsolicited advice.

Yes, you can do it yourself.

The difference is that when you handle the transactions yourself, you pay a very small fee, a reasonable fee. When you go through a broker, you pay a much higher fee. And you get nothing for your money. It's like paying a pimp to set up a date with your boyfriend or girlfriend. Not a very bright idea.

Financial advice? You can get plenty of that on the Internet, most of which you should probably ignore. You are getting financial advice here, at the kitchen table, while enjoying Mom's spaghetti sauce. Unlike the broker, we don't have a hidden agenda to keep sucking you dry. Unlike the broker, we don't charge you extra each time you trade stock.

You might be wondering why Mom doesn't like mutual funds. You usually buy those and hold them for a long period of time, which sounds a lot like Mom's recipe for investing. And with mutual funds, nobody is hoping you'll buy and sell just to earn a commission on the trade.

Well, that is and isn't true. Most mutual funds do charge a transaction commission, either up front or "rear load" (when you sell). So you still do pay to buy and sell, and that payment is generally higher than if you were to buy stocks straight out. So the fee is still higher than if you do it yourself.

But wait! There's more.

I sound like one of those as-seen-on-TV pitches, don't I? "But wait! There's more!" Except that this isn't a pitch; it's a warning. I really should be saying...

"But wait! There's less!"

Mutual funds also have management fees. Yes, you pay a percentage of your investment each year for somebody to manage the fund. Imagine how rich you'd be if you paid someone to manage your mortgage, or your insurance, or your garden, or your sleep. Why do you need a management fee?

A high MER (management expense ratio) means that you have little chance of making much profit. In fact, when considering inflation, you might even take a loss.

A low MER means that you have a better chance of making some profit than you have with a high MER, but you will still make less than if you do it yourself. You know why? Because you are still paying somebody else to manage your stocks rather than paying yourself. If your goal is to make money, not pay money, why would you pay someone else instead of making it yourself?

MERs include a kickback called "trailer fees". These go straight into the pocket of your investment firm. So somebody makes money on the MERs besides the mutual fund manager. Can you guess who?

Think about it.

The stockholders of the mutual fund company. Yes, isn't that ironic? You could make more money from mutual funds by buying stocks of the mutual fund company than by buying the mutual funds they sell, because everybody who buys into a mutual fund is paying the stockholders of the mutual fund company.

Doesn't that take the cake?

Now while Mom clears the dishes – Thanks, Mom. You're the best! – would you like to hear an interesting bit of trivia?

OK, here goes – what else does MER stand for? Can you guess? "Mer" is the French word for sea. In other words, mutual funds are drowning in a sea of extra costs.

There are other options, such as ETFs. "When they were initially introduced, mutual funds were designed to give retail 'mom and pop' investors broad exposure to the stock market and the idea of diversification," says David Bickerton, Portfolio manager at MDH Investment Management, Inc., in Ohio. But he notes that the same exposure to diversification can be gained through exchange-traded funds (ETFs), also sometimes called "index funds", because they roughly reflect the composition and value of a particular index or market segment.

"With the advent of ETFs, investors can get the exact same exposure to the market that they desire for a fraction of the price. Mutual funds often have large sales charges, marketing fees, and administrative costs to the group that manages them whereas ETF fees are usually very minimal," says Bickerton.

With mutual funds, you lose the control. With DIY investing with ETFs and stocks, you don't.

Can I offer you some tea?

Right, now let's get on to another reason why going through a broker is not ideal. First, they don't have your interest at heart, then they charge exorbitant fees for their "service".

THIRD, you get stuck with hidden fees and leeching

But wait! There's less! With a broker, you are paying full tax on any capital growth or dividends payable. Nothing wrong with paying taxes, of course; that's just you doing your share. That's just being sociable and responsible. Nothing wrong with that. But why pay more taxes than you need to when others are paying less?

In Canada, we have a tax-free savings account (TFSA) to which we can contribute each year. In 2015, the upper contribution limit was raised from $5,500 to $10,000. That means you can put up to $10,000 each year into an account without paying tax on any amount it generates within the account.

Here's a riddle for you:

Question: How many financial groupies can you fit into the TFSA?

Answer: All of them. That's right, financial groupies in Canada have been flocking to the TFSA even more than to TGIF.

If you don't have a TFSA, set one up right away. As soon as you leave here, in fact. If you already have a TFSA, convert it right away to an investing account, so that you can buy stocks within that account.

Mom is doing just that right now. She is transferring as much as she is allowed each year into a TFSA.

Above the limits imposed by the government on TFSAs, you can also limit your costs by signing up for online trading accounts at any of the Big 5 Canadian banks.

In the United States, there is no TFSA. Then again, there's not much in the way of taxes in the USA. You can go straight to self-managed online brokerages from any major, federally-insured bank. Nevertheless, it is still best for Americans to follow Mom's recipe. That's because of the preferential treatment of long-term capital gains over short-term capital gains.

A capital gain is the increase in value of anything, including real estate, art, jewelry and, of course, stocks, when they are sold – the profit you make from selling what you bought earlier. Stocks held for less than a year are treated in the United States as short-term capital gains, and a higher tax rate is applied to them. Stocks held for more than a year are treated in the United States as long-term capital gains, and a lower tax rate is applied to them.

You see, the US tax code encourages investment and discourages speculation. Mom also encourages investment and discourages speculation. So to reduce your taxes, make sure to hold onto your stock for at least a year.

In the US. it is also noteworthy that most 401ks do not allow you to purchase individual stocks, which is how most employers supply pensions. However, you can convert your 401k into a traditional IRA (Investment Retirement Account) or a Roth IRA. Yeah, I see your eyes glazing over, but don't worry – I won't get into too much detail on IRAs because Mom didn't prepare the guest room for an overnight.

Both IRA and Roth IRA accounts allow our money to grow tax-free within the accounts. This does not mean you won't pay taxes, but the taxes are deferred. The government wants you to pay your taxes – you noticed that, right? – but they give you ways to delay those payments.

Why would they do such a thing? To encourage people to save and to invest. In the long run, you will pay less tax if you do the things the government wants people to be doing.

But there are rules, rules, rules, and the rate you pay on capital gains might be more or might be nothing, depending on the type of IRA and other financial considerations. Either a traditional IRA or a Roth IRA will provide tax advantages, but it really is worth consulting an accountant or a financial advisor (one who doesn't sell "products") to determine which one will benefit you the most.

I see you look puzzled by the differences between Canada and the USA. If you plan to do a lot of cross-border buying, it's worth consulting a tax expert to at least know the implications of various tools and what strategies allow you to keep the most of your investment profits.

It's enough that mutual funds want to slap you with all sorts of hidden fees and unnecessary costs. You don't need the government or anybody else to come along and add a whole bunch of extra fees on top.

Remember that evading taxes is illegal and Mom and I do not recommend doing that. But we do recommend using the best strategies and legal tools to reduce the taxes you have to pay, as long as you continue to invest smartly, with a disciplined eye toward long-term investments in solid companies. If the government was to offer a tax break tomorrow for people investing in the wrong types of companies or using foolish investment strategies, I doubt we would recommend changing your strategy just to take advantage of the tax break.

Fourth, lower profits

But wait! There's less! (I love saying that.) If you follow Mom's investing recipe, you will rise with the market and fall with the market. Why is that such a good thing? Remember the graphs and tables I showed you at our last session? Remember how even during the decade of the Great Depression, the stock market didn't lose very much value over the medium run? Plus people who held on to their stocks kept earning dividends.

Yes, even when the stock market lost a huge amount of value very, very quickly, people who stayed invested did not lose much for long. People who kept on investing, especially while the market was low, made a healthy profit.

It's great to rise with the market, because the market always does rise. It's OK to fall with the market, because it's always temporary and generally much less of a fall than the rises before and after.

But what if you could beat the market? What if, while all the other suckers rise with the market, you could rise even higher? And what if while they fall, you could hold even or maybe even rise a bit?

What if you could beat the market?

That is a gambler's never-ending dream – to defy the odds and beat reality. And it is fueled by the fact that a few people will get lucky and beat the market. A few people will defy the odds and get crazy rich. There is always somebody who gets lucky, who draws the short straw, who has the winning ticket.

A few other people will also defy the odds and have to dress in potato sacks for the rest of their lives. That's just the luck of the draw. Gambling is not an investment strategy. I don't want to see you sitting around this kitchen table chatting with me in a potato sack.

What you really need to understand is that the market is an average, and there will always be some people who do better and some people who do worse. In fact, they will cancel each other out, right down to the last penny. That's how averages are formed. But if you play it smart, you aren't gambling. If you follow Mom's recipe based on facts, planning and discipline, you will rise and fall with the market. In the long term, you will win.

Remember those three magic words:

- Facts.
- Planning.
- Discipline.

How can you beat the market, when everybody is trying to beat the market? Don't forget who the "market" is. It's all of us. What makes you so special that you can beat everybody else?

Some people think that hiring an expert will give them the edge. In fact, lots of people think that way. On the surface, it makes sense. An expert probably knows what he is doing more than you do, so he can probably beat the market, right?

Not really. You see, most of the people trying to beat the market are "the experts", and they can't all beat the market. The "market" is all of the experts. What makes your expert so special that he can beat all of the other experts? No, seriously. Put aside wishful thinking, fairy dust and that lucky rabbit's foot you just slipped into your broker's pocket.

What makes you think your financial advisor is so special that he can be above average while all the others are also trying to be above average? Try to visualize thousands of people climbing on top of each other to reach the top of a greased pole. I'll give you a moment to visualize that. Yes, that's what all the brokers are trying to do.

They can't all get to the top of the greased pole.

They can't all be above average. The market is the average, and that means – well, think about what average means. It means there is as much above as below, and as much below as above, and if one "expert" beats the market, another "expert" gets beaten by the market. The one you hire might beat the market for you. Or he might get you beaten up by the market. The market is, don't forget, include all the other experts out there.

This is what Timothy W. Holt, Investment Advisor Representative at The Holt Capital Management Group, L.L.C. in Glendale, Arizona meant when he warned against day trading: "Like all gambling, you cannot beat the house. In this case 'the house' is the rest of the market and the investors who are working hard at it." You can't beat the market; that is a gambler's approach, not an investor's."

If you choose to hire a financial advisor, it should not be to try to beat the market; it should be to seek help riding the market and moving up with the market.

But wait! There's less! Interestingly, the majority of mutual funds fail to beat the market and actually underperform.

Did you hear that right? Yes, you did. Imagine if you paid somebody to manage your garden, and you noticed how nicely the weeds were growing. Or you paid someone to manage your mortgage, and suddenly found the Lorax in your basement, because you had to take on a tenant. Or you hired someone to manage your sleep and they kept waking you up to tell you that they are still on the job, at their post, watching over you, tracking your progress, keeping their eye on the ball, and – oh, the Monty Python of it all!

What? What did I say? I see you were listening when I said, "The majority of mutual funds fail to beat the market and actually underperform." If the market is an average, how can the majority of mutual funds underperform, you ask? There should be roughly the same number of over-performers as underperformers, right?

Right. But ... not quite right. OK, think about it. What did we talk about earlier?

Fees!

Yes, commissions and management fees. Even if the investments in the mutual funds break even with the market – which you are absolutely right that on average they should – by the time all the fees are accounted for, you lose. Even if the fund manager beats the market, *you* fail to beat the market. You fail to keep pace with the market. You lose. You gambled, you won ... but you still lost.

You could have invested directly in the market without paying all those fees and most likely kept pace with the market. But you hired a fund manager to keep pace with the market for you. You hoped they could earn you more profits. And even if they do earn you more profits, you cancel it out with the fees you paid them. Would this be a good time to shout out, "But wait! There's less!" again?

Fifth, scams

The system is out to get you.

It's like hiring a professional chef, thinking that you'll get the best tasting spaghetti in the world, but every time he makes it really good, he keeps it for himself.

Every heard of Mitchell Tuchman? He's a Harvard M.B.A. who spent seven years analyzing technology stocks for a hedge fund. Here is what he says about buying mutual funds: "The fees that fund companies and wealth managers charge create inherent conflicts of interest. It's like cigarette makers in the 1930s trying to convince people that smoking was healthy."

Have you ever received an email telling you that a certain stock will go up over the next seven days? Some people get that email.

After seven days, they get another email showing that the stock did go up, and this time, telling them that another stock will go down in the following seven days. At this point, the emailer has your attention.

Sure enough, seven days later comes the email showing how they had predicted correctly. Now you're really paying attention when they identify a rising stock to watch for over the next seven days.

When you see that stock go up, just as the emailer predicted, you are ready to sign on the dotted line. These guys obviously know what they are doing. These guys can beat the market week after week after week. These guys are good!

Actually, these guys are scammers.

How can that be?

Simple. A sketch on a dinner napkin's worth a thousand words!

How They Lead You to Believe Them

They start with a list of let's say 1000, people. They email half of them to say that a certain stock will go up. They email the other half saying that the same stock will go down. After seven days, the stock has either gone up or down, and they discard the email addresses of those to whom they had sent the wrong prediction.

To the 500 who had received the correct prediction, they now send a new prediction. To 250 of them, they say a stock will go up; to the other 250, they say it will go down. Once again, after seven days, they have impressed 250 people, to whom they send a brand new prediction, identifying a stock that will go up to 125 of them and down to the remaining 125.

875 of the 1000 people receiving the original email will not be impressed. 125 of them will sign on the dotted line, falsely believing that the scammer can predict the stock market accurately. In fact, all the scammer can do is play the averages.

And you can play the averages, too, without paying commissions and management fees to do it for you. Mom manages her own stocks without the benefit of a scammer in under an hour per day with a high school education and no special training. It's not complicated. All it takes is a plan, discipline, sticking to the facts and not getting carried away with greed and dreams of beating the market.

And a hot cup of tea. She likes a hot cup of tea.

Sixth, too late to the table once the "experts" have been there

Ah, I see you've brought me the financial pages of the newspaper. Let's take a look. OK, I see this guy is recommending three stocks to purchase. Well, he certainly does have the credentials. He's a broker at a prestigious financial company and he says he has bought into all three of these stocks himself.

Let's call up those three stocks on the computer here. Just bear with me while the pages load. OK, here we go. All three stocks have been on the rise over the last few weeks.

Sounds like good advice, eh? So, what should you do?

Well, I can see by your face that you want to scream out, "Buy!" But you seem to have some doubts. Do you think I'll tell you it's all a scam?

Well, you're right. Oh, I don't mean they are trying to scam you, not as such. But nine times out of ten, you'll lose by following these hot tips. Why? Here are a few reasons:

Unless there is a huge shift in the market, like the company has just secured a patent for something that really will permanently change the sector, chances are that any rapid rise – any increase above the long- term trend – is a blip. It's temporary. Think about what that means. It means that these three stocks, which have already risen quite a bit, are likely to fall in the short term more than they will rise. They are likely to correct themselves to the levels they "normally" would have been.

Mom and I do not recommend trying to time the market. I have said it before and I will say it again. But if you do try to time the market, this would be the time to sell, not to buy. Buying after a stock has been on a tear is a pretty risky move.

So why would this respected financial expert recommend buying? Is he crazy? Of course not. He owns a lot of this stock, right? He bought it. If it's good enough for him, surely it's good enough for you. But now he owns a lot of the stock. Which means that he wants it to keep rising more before he sells it, right? And how can you make stock increase in value? By getting more people to buy it.

So here is how it typically plays out. Financial expert buys lots of a stock when it is low and poised to make a temporary jump. As it starts to rise, he recommends everyone join him to get rich. They do, driving the price even higher. He sells his stock for a nice profit, takes his money, and runs away as fast as he can. Everybody else, still hoping to earn just a little more before they sell, especially the most recent buyers, takes a loss when the stock falls. Here's how these graphs usually look like:

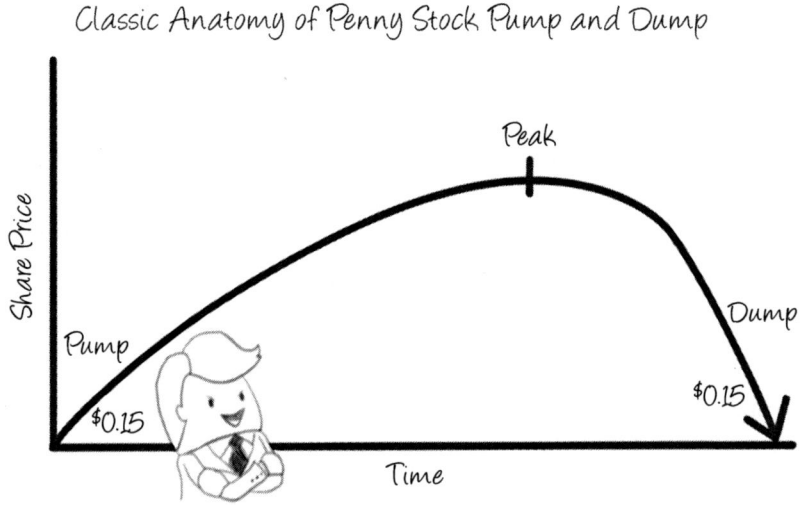

It's like sending you into the strawberry fields after the bushes have been stripped bare. Or like offering you all the oil in a dead well. Or naming you an heir while blowing the inheritance in Vegas.

So what am I getting at? Listening to "expert" advice in the media is worthless. Use hard data and common sense, not opinions and hearsay, even if the opinions and hearsay are cloaked under the guise of "expert advice".

If you are paying for the financial advice, from a certified financial advisor who is duty-bound to have your best interest at heart, that's a different matter. And nine times out of ten, I'll bet he tells you to ignore that hot tip you read about.

Oh, and also don't be a trader. Don't try to time the market. Buy for the long run. Yes, I know, I keep repeating those lines. Please make sure they sink in.

Seventh, nothing new to add

If you don't rely on expert advice in the media or hire a broker or buy into a mutual fund, how will you know what to do?

One of the greatest investors of our time, Warren Buffett, is famous for saying, "Wall Street is the only place that people ride to in a Rolls-Royce to get advice from those who take the subway."

I have already shown you how so much of this "expert" business is an illusion, rife with self-interest that can leave you the loser. The fact is that most of the mutual funds are top-heavy with the very same stocks that Mom buys without the "benefit" of extra advice, a broker on her payroll or a fund manager telling her to invest in them. These are the large cap companies, the name brands that almost anybody will recognize, the kind of companies that one finds in the Dow in the US. If you are investing in the US, those are the main stocks you want to hold.

If you are investing in Canada, there are equivalents. There are the big banks. There are major financial companies like Manulife and Great-West Life. There are large resource stocks like Alcan and Petro-Canada and Suncor and Enbridge. There are other like Rogers Communications and Loblaws.

Check the holdings of most general mutual funds and you will see that the majority of their holdings are stocks from these very same companies that you could invest in yourself without paying management fees so that somebody else can do it for you.

Stock portfolios are like spaghetti sauce, but don't try to eat them (too much fiber, not enough taste). Everybody has their own recipe, but they are all made from the same basic ingredients. Even Mom's special recipe is pretty much the same, once you remove the fenugreek. You don't need to hire somebody to give you a spaghetti sauce recipe. And you don't need to hire somebody to give you a recipe for a stock portfolio. We'll give you the recipe, and you can adapt it in small ways to make it your own.

You can set yourself up with a discount brokerage account and buy the stocks yourself. The fact is that the media darlings and mutual fund managers have nothing new to add. If they brought you value and earned you higher profits, I would recommend you pay close attention. But they don't increase your profits. They just eat away at your profits.

You don't need them. You don't want them. They have nothing new to add.

Eighth, follow facts and your own advice

You will read a lot in the media. Most of it is not fact. Most of it is newspapers and TV trying to spin an exciting story to keep people reading and watching. Sure, there is some actual news in the news, but it is hard to separate fact from opinion, and we humans tend to latch on to opinions when we want to hear them.

That's how we get tricked into buying stock recommended by financial expert commentators, because we trust their opinion. That's how we get tricked into trusting scammers, because we want to believe we can get rich easily. The problem is that we are constantly filtering the news based on what we want to hear.

It's only the facts that count.

I don't care if you want to trust somebody. I don't care who says they have a hot tip, whether it is a famous fund manager, a Hollywood celebrity or the mechanic down at the garage who assured you last week that the noise under the hood was fixed once and for all (again!). I don't care what opinions pass as news. Only the facts count.

Mom learned her lesson with some early investments in penny stocks. They just sounded so good. But that's not fact. That's just opinions. Most people are swayed by opinions. Mom was too. She bought the lines and she bought the GZGT stock. Most importantly, though, she learned her lesson, and I am passing that lesson on to you.

You see why Mom took out the cayenne pepper on out very first meeting when I mentioned penny stocks? Penny stocks are for gamblers, not for investors.

If you follow Mom's recipe for investing, creating a plan and sticking with it for the long run, you'll be able to listen to your own advice. Based only on fact, you can ignore the noise and distractions and marketing that will toy with your emotions and lead you off the path to success.

Ninth, DIY does not mean being alone

I think one of the biggest reasons people hire brokers or buy into mutual funds is because they are scared. Yes, doing something big on your own is scary. You wonder if you can. You are not sure how. Most people like to have support, to have someone else tell them what to do, so that they don't have to make big decisions alone. But investing is pretty easy if you just open a discount brokerage account and follow Mom's recipe.

You are not alone. Mom and I are with you.

And once you buy a stock, there are thousands of other people working to make you money. The company's board of directors, the company's president and vice-presidents and managers and legal counsel and all the people working for that company are doing what they do with one, singular purpose – to pay you. They are working to increase the company's profits so that they can pay you a dividend and so that the value of the company's stock will increase over time.

If you buy stock in a company with a mascot, even the mascot is working for you. That is a pretty poor reason to buy stock in a company, but some solid companies do have mascots. For instance, McDonald's has Ronald McDonald. How cool would it be to tell all your friends that, "Ronald McDonald works for me." On the other hand, if you invest in Fruit of the Loom stock, maybe just keep that tidbit to yourself.

But they all work for you, from the president to the mascot, from the technicians to the file clerks. All you have to do is buy the stock. That's the easy part. Leave the heavy lifting to the employees, while you go shopping or dining or jogging or painting magenta polka dots on all the flowers in your garden. As long as you have chosen common sense stocks the way we'll show you to do, your part is as easy as spaghetti sauce.

If you still feel alone, if you still are nervous, hire a for-fee financial advisor. You don't need one, but at least you should be able to trust their advice.

Tenth, yes you can believe in your own common sense

We all have common sense until we get into politics. And that is all it takes to make smart investments. Stay out of politics and you are half-way there. By the end of our sessions, you will see that everything we are talking about is common sense. Even when I show you some pretty cool things that are at first counterintuitive, you will see that this is all common sense, right Mom?

> *Not everybody sees it right away. But when you put your brain to work, it all makes sense. Yes, it does.*

Exactly. It only gets mixed up when you start listening to the experts with their own agendas. They make it sound so complicated. It's like Mom's Vindaloo Chicken. There are 20 ingredients on the list, and if you just glance at it, you'll be saying, Holy Vindaloo! That looks complicated." But if you look at the recipe, it's really quite simple.

There are only 4 steps, and I'll bet you would laugh to think that it looked so complicated at first.

Brokers and fund marketers do essentially the same thing. They have created complicated systems and their own special lingo because it confuses people like you and me when we just look at it. That's right, they want us to be confused so that we rely on them to sort it out for us (for a nice hefty fee, of course). But we don't need to pay that fee. We don't need them to sort out their own confusion. We don't need their confusion in the first place. All we need is common sense.

That's what Mom's recipe for stock market investing is all about. Common sense, making decisions based on facts, and sticking to the plan. No need for confusion.

Timothy W. Holt says, "The free market economy that exists in the United States today is as real as it was from the days of the Founding Fathers. I don't care who you are or where you came from. If this is something you want to do and you're willing to pay the price, the American dream still exists. Nobody cares what color you are, nobody cares what your last name is, all that matters is your decision-making ability and your willingness to get the information. And that is what this country still stands for today."

And it's the same in Canada. A Chinese housewife with faltering English and relatively little formal education can make serious money working an hour a day on her investments. That's the magic of the stock market.

There are some things you don't want to do yourself. If you need a lobotomy, don't buy a home lobotomy kit; best to call a professional. If your septic tank is clogged, don't crawl inside to investigate; best to call a professional. If you want to fly across the ocean, don't try flapping your wings; best to rely on a professional pilot. Or at least on a very large eagle.

Sometimes, calling a professional is just common sense.

If you want to invest in the stock market, best to NOT call a professional. They really don't bring anything to the table that you don't already have. All Mom needs on her table is this laptop and a fresh cup of tea.

I see our time is up for now, but let me leave you with a challenge. Yes, a challenge!

Before our next session, I want you to buy a lottery ticket. Don't ask why, just do it. Buy a lottery ticket at your local corner store. But don't let a machine pick the numbers for you; I want you to think hard and choose what you believe the winning numbers will be for the next draw. I can go with you to my local corner store to buy it, if you like.

Once you have bought the ticket, remember the draw date and tape it to your bathroom mirror. Once you've done it, great, you've done the challenge. And you don't need a financial planner or mutual fund manager to help you choose that ticket.

> *Here's that fenugreek I promised you earlier. Try it in any pasta recipe. I'm sure you'll love it.*

And remember to set up your TSFA account, as I advised you earlier.

Oh, and don't forget to bring me some of your lottery winnings at our next kitchen table chat ... as a thanks, of course.

WHAT YOU LEARNED ON THIS VISIT

You should manage your own investments.

Brokers have their own agenda, which is not necessarily yours.

Doing it yourself saves a lot of fees and commissions, which means more profits for you.

Brokers don't bring much added value if any at all.

You are not alone. You can always consult a certified financial advisor who is duty-bound to have your best interest at heart.

Facts and common sense are worth more than brokers.

CHAPTER 3
Why Trading Sucks

> *Time is your friend; impulse is your enemy.*
>
> —John Bogle

Welcome back to our humble home. The kitchen table awaits, and I am pleased to let you know that a very special guest will be joining us shortly, a gentleman by the name of Jim Rogers.

Right this way. You know where the famous kitchen table is, with Mom's trusty laptop and ... ooh, what's this? Mom, you've made us some chicken!

> *Vindaloo chicken, Victor. Remember last time you explained how complicated the recipe looked, but how easy it is to make. Well, I made it in under an hour, just like I take under an hour to manage my investments each day. Dig in; it's fresh from the wok.*

This is a treat! Mmmm. Mom, this is as delicious as ever.

So let's take a look at where we've come so far. On your first visit, I introduced you to Mom's recipe. Not her recipe for chicken, but for wealth – for investing. Then we took a look at the stock market and how impressive the long term returns are, even through hard times. And last time we looked at how stupid it is to buy stocks through a broker and how it's just common sense to buy them directly.

And last time we left off with … let me see … oh yes, I sent you off to buy a lottery ticket. Yes, and I am a little sore on that count. You did not even send me any of your winnings.

What?

No winnings? Oh, well I guess that's to be expected. Lotteries are gambling, after all. They are not the best investment are they? That is the point of the exercise – to understand the difference between investing and gambling. The lottery feeds the gambler's never-ending dream – to defy the odds and beat reality. Mom's investment recipe is about investing in reality, not gambling.

We do not gamble.

We do not speculate.

We do not wish and hope and dream.

We don't trade; we invest.

Oh sure, there is nothing that is 100 percent. There is nothing that cannot fall. Rome fell. The British Empire disintegrated. The Great depression lasted a decade. But life goes on and business goes on and a sound investment goes on and keeps going up.

Luck is always a factor. It's just by pure chance that we live on a planet where water is liquid. On every other planet, any water would be ice or vapor. So luck is always a factor. But leaving everything to chance is just not a very smart way to build wealth.

Moms' investment recipe is 99 percent certain. It follows the market. It minimizes costs. The long term is always up. If another Great

Depression hits, you will take some short-term losses, even with everything we tell you. But you will lose less than everybody else in the short term. And in the long term, while gamblers, speculators, and traders are still weeping in their Vindaloo Chicken, you'll already be counting your profits.

Today, I am going to share with you our little secret about trading. OK, so it's not technically a secret, but most financial groupies haven't figured this out yet.

I want you to close your eyes.

Go ahead and close them ...

Oh, for goodness sake, just close your eyes. I won't steal your Vindaloo Chicken while your eyes are closed.

Now picture this. You are looking out over the stock market floor and already it's getting crowded as they wait, bodies tensed for the opening bell. It rings! They are off, grown men in thousand-dollar suits jumping around and waving their arms frantically, yelling and flashing messages in their special sign language, papers flying everywhere with seemingly wild abandon.

No, they aren't geeks that never grew up. They are traders!

You've seen this scene before in movies like in *Trading Places*, *Wall Street* and *The Wolf of Wall Street*. They are worth watching just to see the craziness. The panicking. The pandemonium.

It's like a carnival without the music and the laughter and the fun. But just as crazy and chaotic.

The traders need to act fast. They need to react even faster. Every second could cost them a fortune. They need to buy before everybody else. They need to sell before everybody else. A few seconds late to either buy or sell could spell disaster. And they will keep doing this all day long.

Could the makers of Tylenol and Advil have concocted a more perfect incubation chamber for a captive market if they had tried?

This is high stress. Fighting fires and chasing bad guys seems like downtime compared to trading stocks. A million actions transpire every minute, moving billions of dollars from one set of hands to another. Traders have to be fast, fast, fast.

And they have to be right. Every time.

But they are not right every time and people lose a lot of money that they could have made by just holding on to their stocks for the long term. Making dozens of split-second decisions every minute, moving through a pressure-cooker at the speed of light – that is no way to make long-term investing decisions. That is no way to risk your future.

As Timothy W. Holt puts it, "Search around and you can find someone who was successful, at least on one or two trades. But don't drink the kool-aid they're selling. If you think you understand the odds and that you are smarter than everyone else just look in the mirror. You'll see 'sucker' printed on your forehead."

This kitchen table is not like the stock market floor at all. Here, we are calm and relaxed and, most of all, we are sane. Sane means that we are clear-headed and we can think and we can act in a way that makes sense. Sane means we don't have "sucker" tattoos on our foreheads.

Trading sucks. It is not a sane way to manage our money. Think about this for a minute. If the professionals make split second decisions to time the markets to the second, and still get much of it wrong, how would you compete with that? How would you make a trade in time to beat them out?

Remember that every transaction has a winner and a loser. Somebody buys the stock just as it's about to go up, which means some sucker sold it just before it goes up. Somebody sells their stock just before it dips, which means that some sucker buys the stock just before it loses value. When you go toe-to-toe with these pros, which of you do you think will be the sucker?

You can't beat them at the trading game.

But you don't have to. There are pro chefs who could have whipped up this chicken in half the time Mom did. She can't compete with that. But she doesn't have to. At the end of the day, we have all the chicken we can inhale. And the only regret is that now I have no room for dessert.

Mom's investing recipe is about doing it right, investing for the long term, not about competing with gamblers and traders.

Meet Jim Rogers

I told you that we would be having a very special guest join us. Well, I might have misled you just a little. Jim Rogers won't be physically joining us. But he will be joining us as part of this conversation because I want to talk about Jim.

You see, Jim is a trader.

Did I say Jim is a trader? No, Jim is not just a trader. He is possibly the most celebrated trader of our time. He's a product of both Yale and Oxford, known for his contrarian insights. He was such a successful Wall Street banker that he caught the attention of George Soros. Ah, that's a name you recognize. Soros is certainly a legendary financial whiz. Well, the two of them co-founded Quantum Fund in 1973. In 10 years, the Fund gained 4200%, while most other funds were struggling to make a profit.

So Jim Rogers is somewhat of a whiz himself.

And if past success can predict future success, those six stocks he bet his fortune on in the early seventies would have made him even richer. But instead, they nearly wiped him out.

Here is what he said about that fiasco: "I had nothing left. Four months before I had been brilliant. I had done brilliantly when nobody else was making money at all …. So I knew that I was a genius …. So you can imagine to go from that, that cockiness and arrogance to being totally wrong."

Past success is no indication of future success. In fact, past success can even cloud a person's judgment. When any emotion gets hold of a person, their intelligence tanks. Love will do it. Anger will do it. Fear will do it. And so will euphoria.

Making big decisions in a carnival atmosphere is stupid

Mom never bases her decisions on the thrill of past success. She bases her decisions on the facts. That is discipline, and that is what I want you to do.

The most vulnerable state for an investor immediately follows a huge win. You popped ten balloons in a row with the darts. You won the giant stuffed panda wearing the apron that reads "Frying Panda King". You feel like you rule the world and you make rash, emotional decisions.

Have you ever seen this trick in a movie, or perhaps even in real life? *The Hustler* is a good example of this. So are the robot fights at the beginning of *Big Hero 6*. The pool hustler or card shark enters the joint and plays dumb like he knows how to play the game, but, oh gee whiz and gosh darn, he doesn't think he can really play that well, but my it sure looks like fun, and maybe he'll try it just once. They take his money gladly, but he's had a lot of fun, so he'll maybe try just one more time, and again he loses his money.

But he really would like a chance to win it back, so he pulls out something more valuable – and this time he smokes them and cleans up with a huge pot. Wow! This is amazing. Must be beginner's luck. That was fun. Can we play it again?

And he ends up wiping everybody dry at the end of the night. Why? How does he do it? Why don't the other guys see through his ruse? Simple – they got used to beating him and by the time they were sweating, they already had too much invested that they needed to win back.

Does this sound familiar? Woohoo! A big stock-trading win. Let's try this again. Oops. Lost a bit there. But I know I'm amazing, so I'll just win it back (mix of cockiness and pride with a tinge of fear and worry). And it goes downhill from there.

Learn from Roger's mistakes by not letting your ego dictate your actions, and don't think your past success will determine your future. It only takes a couple mistakes to get wiped out. That's the reality of the stock market; it's a hustler. The stock market of its own accord will hustle you if you let it. Just like the barkers at the Midway. "You get three tries. Everybody gets a prize. You can do it!"

Mom, please take this dish away. Else we'll eat until we explode. It's just too delicious.

Sometimes asking someone to take it away is self-discipline. If the chicken's not there, it won't call out to us. If we don't walk down the Midway, the barkers won't call out to us. If we don't score a lucky trade, the stock market won't hustle us.

Traders get hustled. Investors don't.

If you base decisions on the facts and stick to the plan, you need have no fear. You won't get hustled; you won't even hear the barkers calling to you. Can you show that kind of self-discipline? This is important for you – the very foundation of your success as an investor. Can you show that kind of self-discipline?

Catalysts

In trading, it is easy to get carried away, because there tend to be huge losses and huge wins. Either one can send you on an emotional roller coaster. Either one can cloud your judgement. Either one can make you more of a gambler and less of an investor. Trading sucks.

In trading, there is always a catalyst, a reason for the stock to go higher or lower. That reason might be valid or invalid, or it might have absolutely no effect. Or it could send a wave of panic or make traders tingle with excitement.

Let me give you an example. There is a break-up or a major restructuring of an oil company. Suddenly everybody is whispering that the company is going down sharply or that it is the next big thing. Maybe they are all whispering about how oil will suddenly shoot either down or up as a result.

Whisper, whisper.

Gossip, gossip.

Did I mention not to listen to the opinions of others? Opinions are speculation. Acting on speculation is gambling. Gambling is no way to build a secure future.

These are short term fluctuations in price, based on day-to-day, moment-by-moment news. If you don't have split-second timing, you might buy high and sell low, which is not the way to go.

As I already mentioned, any selling or buying based on split-second timing is dangerous even for the pros, and most likely devastating for you. I'm sorry, but you and I cannot compete on second-by-second transactions. We don't have the expertise, we have no way to get the information as quickly as they do, and we probably cannot carry through a transaction as quickly as they can. There is simply too much going on behind the scenes you don't know about, won't know about and cannot react to in time, even if you did know about. That's why Mom doesn't like investing by buying *options* and *'shorting'* stocks as these methods are information and technique-intensive.

If you guess wrong, you're toast.

If your information is incomplete, you're up in smoke.

If you time it wrong, start digging your grave.

Traders are gamblers, buying on catalysts. Investors don't buy on catalysts.

> *I always buy and sell on solid information that is out in the open and will still be true tomorrow. So I can take my time deciding. I don't have to beat somebody else to the punch.*

That's right, Mom. And what is the magic word you always tell me?

> *You mean facts? Fundamentals?*

That's it, fundamentals. That's the word financial groupies use when they mean the basic, solid information you can count on. Is the market for this product strong? Is the company's brand strong? Do they have enough capital to keep growing? Are their products keeping up with consumer demand? These are the things that count, and these things change over the course of years, not hours or minutes.

> *Buy on common sense and fundamentals, because that's the only sensible way for a small person like me or you to have a fighting chance against the big guys with deep pockets and have faster access to information than we will ever have.*

A lot of people try to get around this minor detail about not having enough information. They read the newspapers. They watch TV. They troll the Internet. They look for any hints as to what the big boys are doing.

They sit on the throne and read what some famous expert has to say.

Business reporters are always asking famous investors and mutual fund managers what stock they are bullish on and what stock they are bearish on. Well, mostly they ask about the bulls. They know their readers are throne-room traders, riveted to their screens, mouths agape and drool freely flowing, desperate for a hot stock tip.

Remember what I told you earlier about hot stock tips? Here is how the process works, in case you forgot:

- The "financial expert" buys stock when it is low and poised to make a temporary jump. His timing is usually pretty good – and if it isn't, you'll never hear about the stock.
- As it starts to rise, he recommends everyone join him to get rich.
- People join him, driving the price even higher as they buy, now for much more than he paid. Their timing ranges from poor (at first) to really, really, I mean really poor after a very short while.
- He sells his stock at a higher price before people wake up and it falls and he makes a nice profit.
- By selling, he helps drive the price down so that the people who took his advice and bought high now take a loss selling low.

The throne-room traders have just been hustled.

No, let's be accurate about it. By even listening to the advice of a broker or investment expert in the media, they have hustled themselves.

Sure you can borrow the knowledge of an expert, but you can't borrow the timing. And in trading, it's all about the catalyst and the timing.

How much is stress worth?

It's no fun being hustled. It's even less fun to be hustled on an ongoing basis. I said earlier that the trading floor at the stock market is a breeding ground for stress, but any trader's life is like that. Even if you trade from the quiet of home, without the carnival and the secret hand signals, you probably won't have any fingernails left after the first week.

Seriously, wear gloves or strap your mouth closed with duct tape.

Have you noticed that each time you come here, all is calm? There're tea and snacks and a clear kitchen table with a laptop on it. Sure, Mom and I get excited about making money. But we do not get stressed.

Even if the market dips.

Even if the market dips really low.

Even if the market is rehearsing for a Limbo competition, you won't see anybody here jumping out of windows. That is partly because we have rose bushes under the windows, and who wants to land in all those thorns? But it is also because we are invested for the long term, and we will continue to make money if we just stay here at the kitchen table.

See this can of cola? That's us. We are sitting here, relaxed and able to focus on our long-term success.

Watch what happens when I shake this can a little. It gets stressed, right? The pressure builds. Let's shake it some more. And some more. In fact, if we shook it for an hour, we might be able to simulate the stress that traders feel. They shake all day long. How do they even sleep at night?

Traders die early. Yes, they get sick more often and die earlier, because that is what stress does to a person. It's been documented over and over again.

But you know what has escaped most people's attention is why people get stressed. Of course, there are many reasons, but some interesting research shows that people in control have less stress. Traders are not in control. They are glued to the bumpers of the catalysts, racing at breakneck speed around hairpin turns. They don't control the catalysts, they can't control the catalysts. The catalysts control them.

We are in control. The market can do whatever it wants today, and we will remain in control while the traders wave their arms and shout their orders and panic and somehow try to unwind when they get home.

We are in control because we have a plan. Because we have discipline. Because the markets won't trick us into following them on a fool's chase.

How much is stress worth? Nothing. In fact, less than nothing. Workplace stress alone has been blamed for $190 billion in healthcare costs each year in the United States. That's not just a monetary cost. "Healthcare" cost means that people's bodies and minds are suffering. They are injured. They are ill. They are in pain.

Remember why investing is so important? So that we don't have to trade our time for money. We get to keep both. Well is it any better if we trade our health for wealth? Of course not. For starters, if we shorten our lives from all the stress of trading, we would be back to trading time for money. More money, less time to enjoy it.

And speaking of enjoying the money, how much will you enjoy it if you spend all your time in and out of doctors' offices and having to watch what you eat. Sure, you can afford any food you want, as long as you don't actually eat it. Could you imagine living a whole life without ever being allowed to eat Vindaloo chicken?

But all that is a moot point if traders don't make more money than investors. An experiment in early 2015 showed that a buy-and-hold strategy of quality companies – eerily similar to Mom's recipe for wealth – massively outperforms the market, even without factoring in dividends. There will always be a select few traders who can outperform the market, as well, but most will fail to do so.

So what if you can't time the market perfectly. What if you don't turn out to be one of the very few super-talented and uncannily lucky traders who make it rich? What if you're just like the rest of us, an average guy who really doesn't make all that much money from trading, despite all the stress involved? What will you end up with?

- A lot of stress.
- Not all that much money.
- Illness, aches, and pains.
- High medical costs and lifestyle restrictions.
- A shorter life, which after being squeezed by pain and the costs of treating it, you might just consider a blessing.

Mom's recipe for wealth is boring. But it works and it is stress-free. Let the traders have all the stress, while the investors like us build our wealth and keep our health. Agreed?

Women have an advantage

Now here's the bad news. Well, it's bad news for me. It's good news for Mom. I'll let you decide for yourself what you think about it.

Women have an advantage when it comes to investing in the stock market. Is it because they are smarter than men?

> *I am not smarter than the average person, Victor. Not man, not woman. But I'm willing to work harder than most are.*

And that's something that is true of a lot of women. Not all, of course, but there are many women willing to work harder than men.

Times have changed and the world is no longer just a man's world. Women are increasingly stepping up in realms that used to be run completely by men. Even at many of the companies we are investing in, there are more and more female CEOs and CFOs and Vice Presidents. A couple decades ago, who would have imagined a female head of the Federal Reserve?

What I am saying is that women are just as capable as men. But there is more. There are a couple character traits that actually give women an advantage, on average. Of course, this does not apply to all women, nor does it exclude all men. But in general, women are willing to work harder … and they are more patient.

> *Patience is very important. It doesn't take any special skill. It relies on your ability to control your emotions and to buy and sell purely based on return without bias. That takes patience.*

Did you hear that word? Control? When we are in control, we have less stress. When we are controlled, we have more stress. The secret to growing your money, also just happens to be control. And patience.

Remember when you first came to visit, I told you how strong Mom is, notwithstanding her bad lower back? This is what I mean. Stock brokers could be running in a panic right outside our window, screaming that the world is coming to an end, and Mom would not sell. Mom is really strong that way. Her goal is to own as many top-quality stocks as possible, not to sell as many top-quality stocks as possible.

Can you be that strong? Can you be that patient?

Any buy and hold strategy requires a lot of patience and a lot of discipline. You have to sit there through reports of doom and gloom on the news and tell yourself, "No thanks, I'll pass. I am in control, not the doom-sayers and the catalysts." Yes, you have to pass on the bad news. You have to pass on the good news. You have to just sit there while everybody else is doing something.

This can be incredibly frustrating for both men and women. But on average, it tends to be harder for men. We, men, are hard-wired for action. We are wired to make things happen, not to just watch and wait while things take their own course. For men, being in control usually means grabbing hold of something physically and moving it.

Men also tend to be more competitive, so they are more likely to feel the need to push things forward, making it harder to just wait and watch. Have you ever noticed, when you are feeling competitive, how you tend to sit on the edge of your seat and are just itching to get in there and play your cards or roll your dice or whatever it is you're playing?

Have you ever noticed how when a ball game is playing on TV, and things are getting more competitive, people can't just sit back and watch? They have to cheer on their team. They wave their hands. They might even jump up out of their seats. They just can't sit still. They just can't do ... nothing.

People get impatient. People feel competitive. People start itching to do something. Some of those people are women, but more often those people are men.

Timothy R. Holt has noticed this, too: "They love being able to brag to their golf buddies about the returns they got in their accounts. When they have a less than stellar year they often change either their advisor or their investment plan and set off in search of 'better returns'." Men have problems in the critical area of patience.

Can you keep calm and remain patient? Can you keep yourself disciplined and stay invested for the long run?

That's what it's all about, being an investor rather than a trader.

Before you go, I want to leave you with a challenge. Yes, another challenge. This one is ... wait for it ... a card trick!

I want you to go home and open a brand new deck of playing cards. Make sure they are well-shuffled. Get a pen and paper to keep track of your score. You are going to turn over the cards one by one, but before turning over each card, you'll have to predict what number or letter the card will be. Don't worry about predicting the suit – just predict the letter or number. With the pen and paper, you can keep track of your score.

OK? Great. I'll see you next time.

WHAT YOU LEARNED ON THIS VISIT

Be an investor, not a trader.

Don't get cocky or impatient; stick to your long-term plan.

Trading is based on catalysts and precision timing.

Trading is high-stress, investing is low stress.

Investors generally make more money than traders.

Women usually have an advantage as investors.

CHAPTER 4
The Profitable Art of Discipline

> *"It's easy to have faith in yourself and have discipline when you're a winner, when you're number one. What you got to have is faith and discipline when you're not a winner."*
>
> —Vince Lombardi

Hello again. Glad you could come back.

Please come in, straight through to the kitchen. You know where the old oak table is by now. In fact, I hope you are starting to feel right at home because today we'll be talking about discipline. And that's, well, a fairly personal topic.

I know, it's not a topic that people usually relate to finances, but it is actually the key to succeeding as an investor. Or maybe I should say, it's the key to not failing as an investor.

What does discipline mean? It means holding firm when an impulse would send you off in the wrong direction. We have all kinds of impulses that sometimes we need to discipline – psychological, sexual, emotional and I see you are resisting an impulse right now. You see Mom's freshly baked coconut balls in front of you.

> *I knew you would be coming over, so I felt like baking up some Lo Mai Chi for you. I hope that's all right.*

Mom, it's perfect. In fact, my mouth is watering. *Lo Mai Chi* has shredded coconut on the outside and crushed peanuts on the inside. They are oh-so-sweet, with a delicate flavour that is to die for. But I think for the moment we'll exercise some discipline.

Yes, sorry. That's cruel, I know. But today is all about discipline.

Just ask any IFBB bodybuilder, professional boxer, or student prepping for the MCAT – they know what I'm talking about. If you are serious about being a successful investor, you too must show discipline.

Last time you were here, we talked about why it sucks to be a trader rather than an investor. We talked about timing, and how tough that can be. We talked about the high stress of trading. We talked about how much more money investors, especially amateur investors like us, typically make.

What is the *REAL* difference between traders and investors?

There is one major difference between traders and investors, and I see you staring at it right now on the table.

No, it's not the *Lo Mai Chi*. Traders can get as much of that as they want, too. It's discipline. The discipline to not eat the *Lo Mai Chi* even though you desperately crave it.

Last time, we talked about patience. I told you that women tend to have more patience, which can be a major asset as an investor. Investments take time to create nice profits, and patience helps a person bide his time.

So what if you don't have patience? Not everybody has a lot of patience, and almost nobody has patience all the time. That's where discipline comes in. Discipline and patience are not the same things. Patience is waiting without feeling the need to lunge forward. Discipline is keeping yourself from lunging forward when you do feel the need to lunge forward.

For instance, I see that you are not patient to taste the *Lo Mai Chi*, and I don't blame you one bit, but so far you have shown discipline and resisted the urge.

You see, discipline can be tough when patience is lacking. Yes, it can be really tough. So let's take a moment to remind ourselves why discipline is so important. Did you do that card trick I asked you to at the end of our last meeting?

You did? Great. Let's see the results.

Hmm.

It looks like you got fewer than one in ten correct. Your guesses were average. You might have guessed better than average. You might have guessed worse than average. But on average, people guess average. That's why it's called "average".

When you rely on luck, there is always the chance to do really well or really poorly, but the laws of probability say that you will probably do average.

The stock market is a lot like that. The moment you sell stock, it could go up or it could go down. You have no way to know for sure.

The moment you buy stock, it could go up or it could go down. Again, you have no way to know for sure.

You could strike it rich! You could be wiped out. But the law of probability says that you will do average, which means that any change in the next few days and weeks after your transaction will probably be too small to jump for joy or break out in tears.

On average, your stock should rise and fall with the market. And as we discussed at our second meeting, that means that over the long term, you should get very wealthy as an investor if you buy good stock and just hold onto it.

But why not buy and sell as often as you want, if on average the laws of probability say that you should do average, which is the same things as rising and falling with the market? Well, there are two reasons:

First, the laws of probability say that you gain nothing by buying and selling, by trading one stock for another. There is simply no point, no advantage.

Let's put it this way: if you look awesome in the blue shirt and you look amazing in the green shirt and you look fabulous in the red shirt, you won't look any better by changing shirts three times in the same day.

Second, the laws of certainty say that you will absolutely pay more fees the more often you buy and sell. Yes, even with a discount online brokerage account, you still pay some transactional fees. The more you buy and sell, the more fees you pay, and the less profit you make. Your stock value might go up over time, but your profits won't.

Like I said, trading sucks.

Discipline is what keeps you from throwing your profits into the wind. You see, if both the trader and the investor earn on average the same amount of revenue from their stocks, but the trader keeps spending that revenue on shuffling his stocks around, who wins?

Exactly.

And stop staring at the *Lo Mai Chi*.

Make a plan to add Mom's special ingredient

The key thing to understand is that you need a plan. And that when you get impatient and feel the urge to mess with that plan, you stick to it. You must show discipline.

The special ingredient you ask? It's *time*.

> That's right, son. Time is the special ingredient I always give my stocks because without enough of it, I just won't see the fruits of my labour. Just like how our young apple and cherry trees in our yard took years before they could bear fruit, so could your stocks.

Yup, don't be a trader, or you'll become a 'traitor'. I hope you laughed at that, or at least smiled. But you heard her, if the stock isn't worth keeping for years and years, it's not worth touching for a second, not even with a ten-foot pole.

First come the facts. Second comes a plan. Third you need discipline. Then you give it time. Always, always, buy for the long run.

So why a plan? What is so special about a plan? If the market rises and falls, but keeps rising over the long run, why not just buy some stock, shove it in a drawer and cash in 25 years later?

Because the market rises in the long run, but not all stocks will rise in the long run. And while nothing is 100 percent certain, there are ways to make the law of probability work in your favour. Mom learned a few lessons through trial and error, and we'll be sharing those lessons with you. That way, you don't have to make your own mistakes.

Yes, you can get something for nothing.

Without a plan, you would be relying on luck, and luck is a gambler's whimsy. No winner in stocks or in anything else relies on luck. Sometimes luck finds a person, but even that is rare. Success is usually the direct result of an effort.

Did you think that the game of Monopoly was a game of chance, just because dice are involved? Sure, there is an element of chance, but there is so much more. Just do a search online for "winning Monopoly strategies" and see how many pages come up. There are some spaces that people land on more than others. There are strategies to pass "Go" and collect $200 more frequently. Even jail time can be manipulated to your advantage. Once you understand the tricks and the strategy, it's hard to lose at the game.

In every game, there are tried and true strategies. That's what our conversations are all about – to share our strategies for stock market investing with you.

Having a strategy does not mean winning every time. You do not become invincible. But it is a lot like entering the wrestling match with your pet grizzly bear by your side. Feel the power!

To rely on luck would be to drop your money on a random stock, without doing proper research and without deciding in advance the buy and sell price to accept.

It's funny, you know. People see others making a fortune in stocks and chock it up to "luck". But that's not usually what it is at all. And if they lose out, they blame it on bad luck, when they simply paid too much for a stock or bought just before it dropped and then sold before it could climb back up.

If luck is an excuse, then that Michael Jordan sure has one super-sized rabbit's foot. So does Wayne Gretzky and Jack Nicklaus.

Now, don't believe all that whining and whimpering. If you want to rely on luck, buy a lottery ticket. I'm not in stocks to make excuses; I'm here to make money. How about you?

You are responsible for your own success, and only you can make it happen. There is no such thing as luck or as fair or unfair. There are only actions and consequences. Take the right actions, and you will get the best available consequence. It's really that simple.

Mom's recipe is about taking the right actions. You need to start with a plan.

The plan, however, must be a sensible one in which you can realistically reach, yet have enough challenge in it so you don't fall asleep. That is the key thing to remember. It is not random. It is not concocted in the frenzy of high emotions. That is the value of a plan. Emotions don't make the best choices, which is why the plan has to be made away from any emotional triggers. All too often emotions drive us out of good investments and into bad ones.

> *Since I had zero stock market knowledge, the one thing I could depend on was my common sense, and a lot of day to day things I do as a housewife have taught me how to be successful in the market. Most of all, I have learned the value of discipline and how to apply it to the stock market through raising a family.*

Right, Mom. So common sense has to rule. This is money we are talking about, so we have to make decisions based on logic, not emotions.

Because she had no knowledge of it, Mom studied the movements of the market for years before she started. What she discovered was this: day to day movements are based on the unpredictability of how people react to the market. Yes, daily volatility is based on how people let emotions control them. No logical explanations can predict how the market moves in the short run, over the course of hours or days. That's why even the best and brightest, with their ears closest to the ground, have so much trouble timing the market.

George Soros laughs at the idea of predicting the market. You know what he said? He said, "The financial markets generally are unpredictable.... The idea that you can actually predict what's going to happen contradicts my way of looking at the market."

That's why trading just doesn't make sense.

But over the long run, over the course of even just a few years, market fundamentals almost always take over to reveal the true value of a stock. That is why so many more people lose by betting on the short run than people like us who focus on the long term. Because the long term is almost always sunny and bright.

So focus on the long run. Make a plan and stick to it. Don't get distracted by short-term fluctuations and all the emotions tied up with those distractions. That is when discipline will make or break your investment strategy.

Just do the opposite

Some people panic when their stock goes down. Emotions take over and they sell. I remember one day when I noticed that one of my stocks had dipped, Mom asked me, "Why are you so concerned when your stock goes down? It's the stock giving you an opportunity to buy more."

> *It's true. If the fundamentals are there, you know the stock will keep rising. A dip in price is the chance to buy more at a discount and make more money.*

I know, I know. If everybody else is selling, shouldn't you be selling, too? This is kind of contrarian thinking, but you really should be doing the opposite of the crowd. Usually, when everybody is selling, that's a great time to buy. And when everyone else is buying, that's a great time to sell.

There's a great quote by General George Patton, and it goes like this: "If everyone is thinking alike, then somebody isn't thinking."

Here's another great quote by Warren Buffett: "I will tell you how to become rich. Close the doors. Be fearful when others are greedy. Be greedy when others are fearful."

Here's one from David Bickerton: "Where there's a crash there's fear and that's where opportunities present themselves."

OK, enough quotes for now. I don't know what came over me. But do you know what makes people like Warren Buffett and George Patton so successful? They don't follow the crowd.

What about most people? They *are* the crowd!

So what's it going to be? Will you be successful? Or will you be the crowd?

I have a story to tell, and it has nothing to do with finances. But it has everything to do with psychology and how people react to things.

Back in my university days, I spent a lot of time going to clubs and partying it up with friends. That's what people do when they are young and free.

I met a guy named Jerod at a club one night. At first, he seemed like just a regular guy. Every week we went to the same club, and after a while it was clear that there was something special about him; he was always surrounded by women. OK, it did not take all that long to notice this. He constantly had beautiful women all over him, and that's not something a guy could miss.

Then one night, a rare occasion when I found him by himself – well, he was urinating, yes, in the washroom, thank you – I couldn't help but ask him what his secret was. I bought him a beer and we chatted a few minutes. That night I received what was probably the most inspiring advice I ever got from a stranger.

He said, "I ain't that rich or anything, but what I do is I do the opposite of what every guy does when they meet beautiful women. Imagine yourself being an attractive woman in a club, how many times will you hear a guy give you compliments and ask 'Can I buy you a drink?' Your brain will eventually filter out those guys. Now when you meet them, instead of being like the other hundred guys who do and say the same thing, say something like this in a jokingly confident manner 'Hey I like your dress. I bet they make it in your size. ' or 'Did your seeing eye dog pick that out for you?' Immediately, you create a sense of curiosity and challenge for her, you stand out and her attention will be fully on you. Most guys wouldn't even think or have the guts to say something like that to a beautiful woman, but that's why it works. To be successful, just do the opposite of what other people do."

Most people act on emotions, and emotions are about your own perceptions. They can be tricked and toyed with, whether on purpose or just by happenstance. If you have a goal, whether it relates to romance or finance, you have to filter out the emotions and focus on the goal. You have to focus on the facts. You have to focus on what will work. And that is often the exact opposite of what everybody else is doing based on their emotions.

Let me give you another example. When you tip a waiter or a bartender, do you tip at the end of the night? Most people do. And it's a great strategy if your goal is to make sure people get what they deserve, no more and no less.

But if your goal is to get great service, try tipping early. I always tip generously on my first drink. Guess what my second, third and fourth drinks are like? They are stiffer. They are filled to the brim. The bartender knows my name and I know his. I get speedier service and I look good in front of my friends. Tipping later on doesn't have the same effect.

Go ahead and try it out the next time you want service. It works in bars. It works in hotels, too. Tip well on your first chance, and for the rest of your stay, the staff will treat you royally. You have to tip early. But this is the opposite of what most people do, and that is why it is so effective.

So what should you do if the market takes a dip and the media are rubbing the word "bear" in your face? How do the reports of how grim the situation is make you feel? How do the reports of how everybody should sell their stocks make you feel? How do the reports of how this time it could be The Big One make you feel? It doesn't feel too good, does it?

I can tell you – it feels horrible. There's a knot in your stomach; I've felt it myself. You watch your stock fall five percent. Then ten percent. Then fifteen percent. When will it stop? It keeps falling! That kind of thing can bring even the toughest guys on Wall Street to their knees. What can li'l ol' you do?

First, you can turn off the TV or the Bloomberg app. Already the pain diminishes.

Second, you can get up off your knees and shout out, "Bull! The panic is a lot of bull. The negativity is a lot of bull. It's all a load of bull!"

You get online and turn that bear into a bull.

When markets dip, that's the time to buy, not to sell. Buy some new stock or buy more of some stock you already own. Anything that dips is a great candidate for buying, as long as the fundamentals are sound. Really the toughest part is turning off your emotions.

We humans have emotions, and they are a beautiful thing. You want emotions like love and happiness, and even fear and anger are important. But never, ever let emotions drive goal-oriented activities like stock investments.

You know where the term bullsh*t comes from? The term comes from people who have a lot of things to say in a *bull* market:

> *Hey, check it out, I just made $4000 in a week from this stock...*

Or

> *I'm telling you, Fred, now's the time to get in! The stock ain't coming down! It's gonna double!*

When you hear this kind of stuff, it's time to turn around and walk away. It's called bullsh*t for a reason. People who have discipline don't listen to bullsh*t or bearsh*t for that matter.

The graph I've drawn on the next page illustrates the relationship between market opportunity and your emotions.

You will discover that people react in fear, desperation, panic, capitulation, and despondency as the market slumps deeper and deeper. And people react in optimism, excitement, thrill, and euphoria as the market rises.

So what should you do?

The Market is an Emotional Roller Coaster

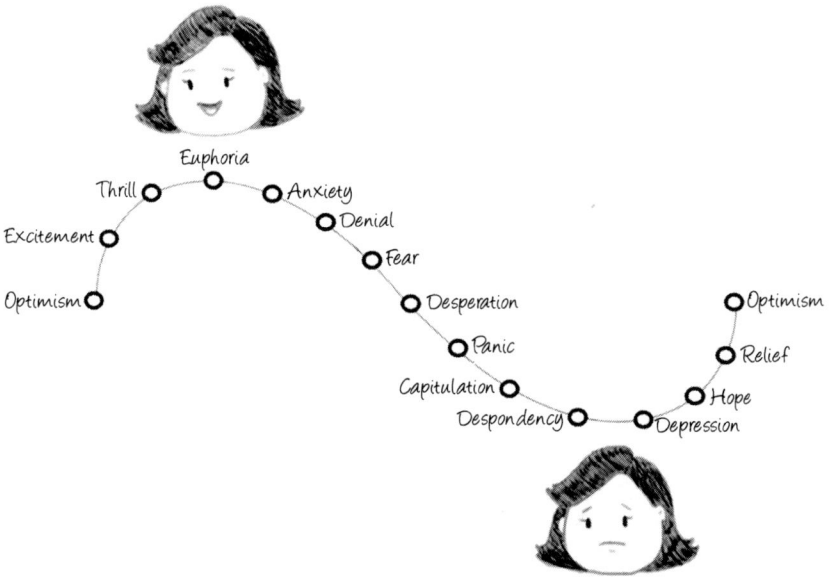

As the market goes higher and higher, good opportunities start to vanish, which is really the market telling you to SELL. When the market turns around and goes lower and lower, good opportunities start to appear, which is really the market telling you to BUY.

So why do people get so easily swayed by emotion? For starters, most do not have a plan. You can't stick to your plan if you don't have one. And without a plan to follow, emotions become incredibly easy to follow.

> *I've always stuck with my plan no matter how dire. It has been a very effective strategy for me.*

Exactly. And Mom sets up target prices for each of her stock. She sets a sell price, and when the stock reaches a certain level, she sells the number of shares she planned to. She sets a buy price, and when the stock dips below a certain level, she buys the number of shares she planned to. She sets these price points well before she even buys the stock.

So always ask yourself, where is the market currently on this chart? It will tell you whether or not there are good opportunities out there.

And well before you arrived, she planned to make us some *Lo Mai Chi*. I think our mouths have watered long enough, don't you? Let's dig in!

Why does the average investor underperform?

So many people lose money because fear makes them sell at the wrong time. People get shaken off before the stock has a chance to regain its value, so they sell it for a bargain. They buy high and sell low. Don't let that happen to you.

Now here is something interesting. Take a look at this report. It's the 2014 edition of Dalbar's *Quantitative Analysis of Investor Behavior* – or QAIB[6]. It says that the average investor with a mix of equities and fixed-income mutual funds has been earning only 2.6 percent per year over the previous decade.

Over the past 20 years, this average investor has been earning only 2.5 percent per year.

And over the past 30 years, this average investor has been earning only 1.9 percent per year. That doesn't even keep up with inflation.

Check out these numbers:

The average inflation rate per year from 1990 to 1999 was 3 percent. And from 2000 to 2009 it was 2.56 percent. That's more than the average investor is making.

Just who is this pathetic "average investor"? Hold on to your socks, your hat and anything else that isn't tied down. This one will floor you.

---

[6] You can access to order the full QAIB report at *www.QAIB.com*

The QAIB report describes the average investor as "the universe of all mutual fund investors whose actions and financial results are restated to represent a single investor." This universe would include:

- Individuals like you and me.
- Pension funds
- Professional investors
- Financial planners
- Our neighbours who buy financial products from brokers

Anybody who invests in mutual funds. Yes, everyone who invests in mutual funds underperforms, including the pros. That's enough to make a person eat another *Lo Mai Chi* … so I think I will. Help yourself. There are plenty, and aren't they delicious? I know!

Remember a couple visits ago when I said, "The majority of mutual funds fail to beat the market and actually underperform." Now you see the result of buying mutual funds. The average mutual funds investor has just barely kept ahead of inflation, and those who have invested exclusively in fixed-income funds have actually lost to inflation. They probably would have been better off just putting their money in a high-interest savings account.

I don't bring up the QAIB report just to rehash the point I made a couple visits ago. The really interesting part of the report is in the "Why?"

Why does the average investor fall on his face? According to QAIB, it is because investors make illogical decisions based on emotions like fear and greed. And that clearly shows that the mutual fund managers are just as human and "unprofessional" as the rest of us. Selling when they should be buying and buying when they should be selling.

Here is how Tom Weary puts it: "Why is there such a big difference between the market returns and what investors were actually getting?

After all, aren't they investing in the markets? The cause of this is due to investor behavior. People buying high and selling low, shooting themselves in the foot. I think it's absolutely vital to have discipline to protect your portfolio, even from yourself. It's true also for professional investors and portfolio managers too, we're all human, and you're just going to do some wrong things at the wrong time."

We can't rely on professional financial planners and we can't just wing it. In either case, emotions interfere. We need to make a plan. We need to stick to the plan. We need discipline.

When a stock value falls, people think they have lost money. In fact, they have not. Only when they sell do they lose anything. Until then, they still have the shares they purchased. They have not lost a single share. If they bought good stock based on sound principles, they should have nothing to worry about. Just hang onto that stock until its value rises. Then when you sell, you will make money.

On the other hand, if they bought speculative stock based on hearsay and wishful thinking, maybe they should sell the stock and cut their losses. But this decision needs to be made on fact, not on emotions.

One of the biggest mistakes that investors make based on emotions is to think they are special. They make this mistake only once. Well, actually they might make it several times, but once it bites them, they don't usually make that mistake a second time.

As we learned with the card trick, on average, people guess average. That's why it's called "average". Unless you have some secret super power I am not aware of, or a time machine hidden away in your garage, you are average. I am average. Even the pros are average.

Remember how we met Jim Rogers in our previous chat? He was the best. I mean, he had the golden touch. He knew it, too. And that was the problem. He thought he was special. I'm not saying he wasn't good, but he certainly had a lot of luck on his side, too.

It took being nearly wiped clean to wipe out that special feeling. Once he realized that he was as human as the rest of us, without any super power, he was able to separate the luck from the skill, and he turned out to be pretty good, after all.

I made the same mistake once. I thought I was special. Up until the 2008 crash, I had been doing quite well. When you succeed, several times in a row, it really boosts your ego. Ever heard that Charlie Major song: "It can't happen to me"? Well, it can. Disaster will strike eventually, and it's how you deal with it that counts.

Why you should love a crash

Just as anybody's house could be wiped out by an earthquake or a satellite falling out of the sky, markets can get hit by a full-scale disaster. I have told you that markets always go up in the long run. But that is only if they survive. According to a paper by William Goetzmann of the Yale School of Management and Philippe Jorion of the University of California, only five countries have survived without a major break in stock trading since 1921.

- The United States
- Canada
- New Zealand
- The United Kingdom
- Sweden

That the UK didn't suffer a major break, even through two World Wars is nothing short of miraculous. One in three countries had to shut down their stock markets permanently – for more than just a few years – due to war, invasion or revolution.

But as long as markets remain open, they inevitably go up. It has always been that way. And there is every reason to believe that it will continue that way.

When the market crashed in 2008, I panicked along with most people. I liquidated my assets. Yes, I sold most of my stock, fearing that the market would sink further. I wanted to preserve what equity I had left. Instead, I locked in my losses.

In the aftermath of 2008, the stock market climbed right back up and soared past the highs of 2007 within four and a half years. That was when I did my research, the research I shared with you on our second meeting. I went back as far as I possibly could and found that through every recession, no matter how big, no matter how small, the markets always emerged triumphantly.

Can you follow me on this train of thought? Markets have always existed for two reasons. They exist to fund projects companies want to undertake. And they exist to create wealth for stockholders like you and me.

If companies ever stopped wanting to do things, markets would no longer exist, because it would not be much of a market with only shareholders offering investment funds to nobody.

If we – folks like you and me – ever stopped wanting to create wealth, markets would no longer exist, because it would not be much of a market with only companies seeking investment funds from nobody.

But as long as there are companies that want to do things and people who want to make money, the markets will always exist. This is one of those 99.9999 percent things we must assume is true, the same way that we must assume we will not get run over by a truck when out shopping. If you're so darn afraid of that truck running you over, then why leave your house at all? Run back into your house, lock your doors and call on the spirits to protect you from trucks falling through your roof and breaking in through the windows.

My point is this: if you are deathly afraid that the market will shut down and all your money will be lost, this is not a realistic fear, but more of a phobia. Because the market is always there. It doesn't just fold up and throw in the towel because things look rocky at one point or another.

Before investing in the market, we must assume that there will always be a market, despite politics, despite social upheaval, despite natural disasters, despite your favorite sports team being devastated year after year. The stock market will prevail. North American markets have proven their resilience.

What I am sharing with you now is … kind of personal. I learned an uncomfortable lesson. What I learned was this: I was soft. I was not tough enough to stomach the crash. Above all, I did not possess the discipline to stay in the market. All I could see and feel were the emotions – the waves of panic and desperation that swept across the market like a windstorm across the Sahara, wearing me down like a million grains of sand.

I had forgotten the golden rule. I had forgotten to remove emotion from the equation. I said things to myself like, "Oh, I never should have chosen these stocks at the beginning" and "it's just really bad luck I have". Like everyone else, I began throwing stocks away to the sinking market, selling them for whatever price I could get. My goodness, what a mistake that was. I see this now in hindsight. I should have been tough. I should have held on. And instead of selling like everyone else, I should have been buying. And I should have listened to Mom.

> *You know, I told him. I said, "Don't blame the stocks, Victor. Blame instead on how you handled the situation. There's nothing wrong with your stocks. The fundamentals are all there. Your stocks are resilient. Don't panic. The market will correct itself soon enough."*

I learned the hard way that discipline has everything to do with investing. I learned that investing *is* discipline, plain and simple.

Peter L. Brooks, President of Brooksie Portfolio Management Advisors, Inc., in New York considers discipline to be a critical character trait for investing: "Over the longer term one needs to have confidence in their judgement when taking a position, otherwise one will lose the necessary stability of mind to correctly stay in the position or get out.

I also learned that a crash is your friend. I mistreated that friend. I sold stock in my panic, and so I lost a lot of the stored value that my stocks would soon regain. I should have bought. The crash was a buying opportunity because so many other people were panicking and selling off their stocks at a bargain. Instead of selling at a bargain, I should have bought at a bargain.

So, you see the importance of discipline?

I know better now, and I have the discipline. I don't make the same mistake twice. I am telling you this so that you don't make that mistake even once.

If you've been reading between the lines, you might surmise that maybe not everyone has what it takes to invest in the stock market. Maybe not everybody has enough discipline. Do you?

Yes, that does sound like a great segue into a challenge, because our time is almost up and so are the *Lo Mai Chi*, and I don't want you to get bored until we next meet. So here is what I want you to do.

For the next seven days, I want you to do a seven-minute workout when you get up in the morning – the very first thing. I don't care what kind of exercise you do. It can be 7 minutes of push ups, sit ups, jumping jacks … whatever. Just make sure that it's intense. It can be a mix of different exercises, that's fine, too. You might want to download the "7 minute workout" app on your phone. The point of this challenge is to find out for yourself if you have the discipline it takes to be successful investing in the stock market.

I look forward to seeing a new, fitter you when we meet again.

WHAT YOU LEARNED ON THIS VISIT

Discipline is critical to stock market success.

Always add *time*, Mom's special ingredient, to stocks.

You need a plan, and you need to stick to it.

Success often comes from doing the opposite of what the crowd is doing.

The average investor underperforms.

Most opportunities are created from a crash.

CHAPTER 5
Universal Truths

> *OCTOBER: This is one of the peculiarly dangerous months to speculate in stocks. The other are July, January, September, April, November, May, March, June, December, August, and February.*
>
> —Mark Twain

Coming! Coming! Just hold on, I'll get the door.

Well, there you are. I am so glad you're back. Am I looking at the new, fitter you? Well, never mind. It was only a week, and it takes longer than that to become fit. Let's go to the kitchen.

I assigned you that exercise just for you to test your discipline. You can keep doing them, too. In fact, you should keep doing them.

What are you looking for? Ah ... you really liked the *Lo Mai Chi* last time, didn't you? Well, none today. Mom's been very busy this week, and just has not had a chance to bake.

Tea?

Last time you were here, we talked about discipline. This time, let's talk about truth. Mankind has always been on the search for truth. Even the US Declaration of Independence is in on the act. The second paragraph, says:

"We hold these truths to be self-evident, that all men are created equal, that they are endowed by their Creator with certain unalienable Rights, that among these are Life, Liberty and the Pursuit of Happiness."

The fact is that there is nothing self-evident about it; since the beginning of time, people have been born into slavery.

We assume that gravity is a universal truth, yet we understand that the physics of gravity is no more than the natural attraction of two objects.

My point is that there are many things that seem so true, that they might as well be universal truths. We can argue them and debate them, but at the end of the day, we still treat them as universal truths. And mankind lusts after these truths.

Studying Mom and her investment recipe is a lot like studying physics. I wanted to learn if there are any universal truths, like liberty and gravity, in the stock market world. The short answer is "yes". If you understand these truths, you can make use of them for your own benefit.

Markets will always exist

On our last visit, I explained why the markets will always exist. This is in fact, the first universal truth. As long as there are people who want to do things, they will need capital. To get that capital, they reach out to people who have capital. That's why they list themselves on stock exchanges.

As long as there are people with capital who want to increase their wealth, they will keep investing in those projects listed on the stock exchange.

That's what a market is, two parties coming together to exchange what they have for what they want. This is true of the local fruit market where Mom buys her tomatoes and mangoes and apples. This is true of the stock, too. The market will always exist.

I won't belabour this point. We talked about it last time quite a bit, and before that, we saw how even the Great Depression didn't do more than dampen the stock market. The markets are resilient, and they will always exist. Let's look at a few other universal truths.

Money loses value

The reason we need to invest is that money loses value. That is the corrosive power of inflation. Year after year, decade after decade, the markets go higher and higher as money consistently loses value.

This is one of those universal truths.

By way of example here is a US $20 bill, which is just paper. It's pretty much worthless, except that the government has printed "$20" on it.

And here is a 1965 Kennedy silver half dollar. Yeah, I know; it's pretty cool to have one of these. This is honest money because it's made of silver. It has real, intrinsic value.

Back in 2003, a $20 bill would get you 28 of the silver half dollars for the silver in them. Not for the face value, of course. It would get you 40 of them for the face value. In 2004, the same $20 would get you 22. In 2005, just 20. In 2006, 12. 2007, only 10.

By 2008, it's down to the silver in 8 silver half dollars for the silver. For the face value, a $20 bill would still get you 40 of the silver half dollars, because inflation would devalue the silver coins' "legal tender" value at the same rate as the paper money. The difference is that the silver coin still holds intrinsic value because it is made of silver. To get a nice visual, let me sketch this out for you:

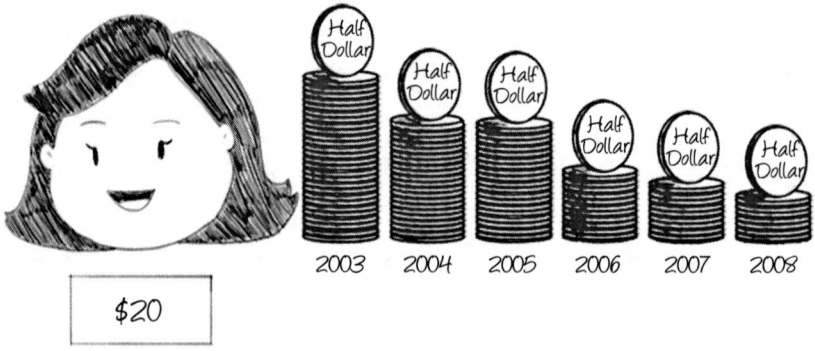

Most consumers see inflation in the price of goods they purchase. In 1944, a bottle of Coke cost 5 cents. What is the price today? In 1955, a Macdonald's cheeseburger cost 19 cents. What is the price today? We grumble about how the price of everything keeps going up, but that's not quite true. It's not the price that goes up; it's the value of the money that goes down.

Our currency is designed to devalue over time because of its very nature – it's printable.

It's the law of supply and demand. The more there is of something, the less valuable it is. So if there is a bumper crop of something in a particular year, you sometimes see farmers destroying some of it in order to fetch a better price.

On the other hand, if demand rises, so do the prices. In fact, that's what a bidding war is all about – when there are more buyers than sellers. You see this in real estate occasionally. You see this at auctions. You see this when the only apple Danish is grabbed before any of the raspberry Danishes surrounding it. You see this when there is one pretty girl in a room full of boys.

Why have our financial markets risen so much over the past century and continue on this upward trend? It's because the more money the government prints, the less that money is worth. Investors need a place to protect their money from this invisible force, which in turn keeps investors pouring money into the markets. The markets' returns are necessary for investors to combat the inflation created by the printing of money.

What about deflation, you ask? Well, yes, that can happen. If there is deflation, money actually grows in value. In the last 100 years, this happened during only one decade, the 1930s. Deflation averaged 2.08 percent per year, which means money gained that amount in value. But over the past 100 years, the average annual inflation rate was 3.22 percent[7]. So money has been losing value at the rate of 3.22 percent per year, even when factoring in the 1930s.

Why does this truth matter?

Because if you want your money to increase in value, it has to increase by more than inflation. Remember last time we met, we saw how mutual funds investors make typically between 1.9 percent and 2.6 percent per year. Some a little more and some a little less, of course, but that is the range of averages.

In other words, it is pretty rare that somebody will actually make any money with mutual funds. In most cases, they will lose money because the value of their portfolio rises less than the rate of inflation. They might earn 2.6 percent in money – Yay! – but that money is now worth 3.2 percent less – Booooo.

Let's keep this simple truth in mind when looking later on at what kind of stocks to buy. Money loses value, and you have to beat inflation if you want to actually get ahead, which is why the worst investment is not making one. Beating inflation can be done, quite simply, and we will discuss that in a future chat.

---

[7] Figure based from the period 1913-2013. *http://inflationdata.com/Inflation/Inflation_Rate/Long_Term_Inflation.asp*

More tea?

Another universal truth is that if you keep drinking tea at this rate, I'll have to show you where the bathroom is pretty soon.

Stocks go in only three directions

Stocks can go in only three directions over time. Up. Down. Sideways.

What? Of course they can go zig-zagging, but that doesn't count as a direction. That's just confusion.

Stocks cannot go backwards because time moves only forward. Tomorrow, your stock will be either higher, lower or the same. Yes, even if they did zig-zag along the way to get there. Higher is great. Lower sucks.

The same sucks, too, because of inflation, remember? Except for dividends. If dividends are high enough, even just staying the same can be good.

Remember when we looked at the Great Depression a few visits ago? People who held on to their stock profited. This was partly because the stocks rose again to a higher level. It was partly because of deflation, which actually increased the value of any savings, including stocks. It was partly because they bought stocks while they were "temporarily" low, and profited when they regained their natural value. But it was also because they continued to collect dividends throughout the Depression.

Find this confusing? Well, it is. The really important question is not whether a stock goes up, down or sideways in actual value, but whether it goes up, down or sideways compared to inflation. But regardless, somebody always makes money.

When a stock goes up, people make money. Those people are the owners of the stock who sell high.

When a stock goes down, people make money. Those people are the watchers of the stock who buy low.

When stock goes sideways, nobody makes money except the brokers.

So as long as a stock moves money can be made, and that is a universal truth.

Stock can't fall below zero

It is comforting to know that zero is the lowest that a stock price can fall. It cannot go lower. You cannot go into debt from a bottomless stock pit. If the price of the stock you buy goes to zero, you will only lose 100 percent of the money you invest – that's it. A stock can never fall below the price of zero.

This is a universal truth.

No matter how wrong you can be about a stock, it cannot fall below zero. But it can go to zero. Any stock can, no matter how good a stock seems. It is within the range of possibilities, so accept it. It's almost like embracing death ... except that it is not inevitable.

Most Canadians probably remember the story of Nortel Networks, which eerily enough resembles the story of Icarus. This company had wings. It had become a globetrotter, signing deals all over the place. With over 94,000 employees, Nortel accounted single-handedly for more than one-third of the capitalization of the Toronto Stock Exchange in 2000. It was unquestionably the safest investment in Canada. Let's face it, if Nortel was to fall, the entire stock exchange would fall, and Canada with it.

But Nortel did crash. Within two years, the stock plunged to about 1 percent of its 2000 value. The safest investment in Canada left everybody injured – yes, that includes all the big pension funds and all the Canadian mutual funds. Everyone went down together.

The sooner you accept that any stock can fall to zero, the sooner you can let go of fear and be confident in the market.

By the way, I should point out that even with the fall of Nortel, the stock market did not fold. Canada did not fold. And people who remained invested in the market are richer today than people who did not. Just saying.

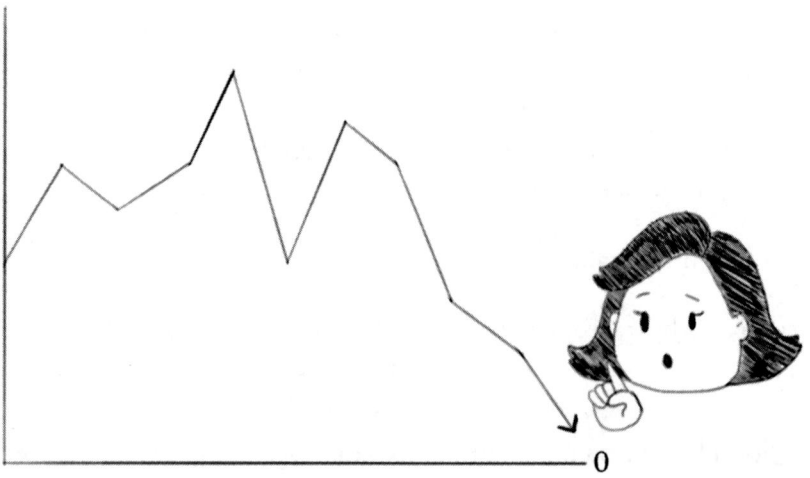

Stocks can't fall below zero. The importance of this truth is simple. Never invest more than you can afford to lose, because it is possible to lose it all.

Now, here's the tricky part. Some fools borrow to buy stock. No! Don't do that! If the stock goes to zero, you will lose it all – all your money that you put in PLUS all the borrowed money that you put in. And you will have to keep paying interest on the loan. So even after the stock falls to zero, you continue to lose money. That means that you will have lost more than 100 percent of the money you can afford to lose.

What? You want to be swimming with the fishes? Don't be a fool! Don't borrow to invest. You'll be breaking a universal truth. You'll be throwing the space-time continuum off course.

OK, maybe it's not that bad. But it is plain stupid to borrow money to buy stocks. You're moving away from investing at that point, and getting into gambling. Nothing wrong about gambling, of course. It can be fun. But even in gambling, the most important piece of advice you will hear over and over is to set a limit, and never put on the table more than you can afford to lose. You don't borrow money to go to the casino. When you borrow to buy stocks, you are putting on the table more than you can afford to lose.

The good news is that a stock can shoot up as far as it likes. There is no ceiling. There is no limit. If you pick wisely, the sky is the limit.

What an awesome system that puts a limit on your losses and no limit on your profits!

Sure, help yourself to more tea. I think that's all we have, though. Sorry, some things have limits.

There is no bad time to invest

Now, some times are better than others to invest, if you can time them perfectly. But as we have already seen, timing the market is a fool's game. The time to invest is when you have the money to do so. It doesn't matter if there is an election on its way or a war is breaking out, or if all the pundits are down on their knees before the Bull of Wall Street.

According to an S&P 500 index analysis done by Ben Carlson, a portfolio manager and finance writer, even if you were the world's worst market timer over the past several decades, you still would have made money in stocks.[8]

In order to illustrate this, Carlson named his unlucky investor "Bob." Bob made 4 lump sum investments in total – all of which at market peaks. His first was $6,000 in 1973, right before a 48 percent crash

---

[8] http://awealthofcommonsense.com/worlds-worst-market-timer/

for the S&P 500. Bob held onto every share he purchased, saving a total of $46,000, and invested it in September 1987—right before a 34 percent crash. Bob then continued to hang onto his holdings, making two more investments, $68,000 which came right before the 2000 crash and then $64,000 before the 2007 crash.

So how did Bob do after 4 decades of market punishment? He ended up a millionaire! As the market continuously reached record highs, Bob turned the $184,000 he invested over the years into $1.1 million—for a total profit of $916,000. That's an annualized return of roughly 9 percent, congruent with the market's 100-year average return. Even after accounting for inflation, Bob's wealth has increased substantially by investing in stocks.

S&P 500 1950-2015

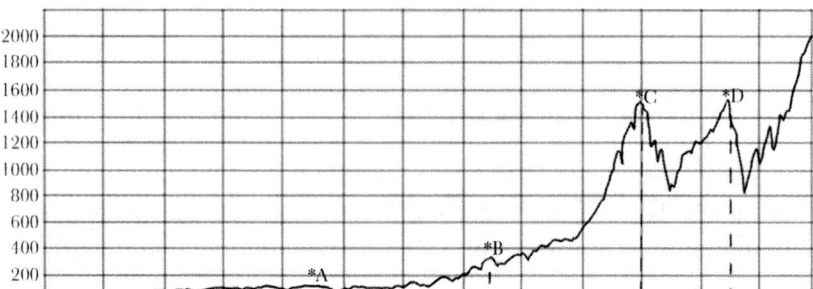

*A – $6,000 in 1973
*B – $46,000 in 1987
*C – $68,000 in 2000
*D – $64,000 in 2007

So what can we take away from Bob's story?

The worst investment is not making one. The worst time to invest is never.

The fact is that there is always a great reason to panic if you want one. There is always some world catastrophe happening that slows the market down. There is always a natural disaster or a political scandal or a mass killing or a company restructuring. In case you need to panic, here is a list to help you. Or, if you want to see how many panic-worthy events have not destroyed the markets, use the same list:

1934	The Great Depression still underway
1935	The Great Depression still underway
1936	The Spanish Civil War
1937	The Great Depression still underway, keep panicking
1938	War appears likely in Europe
1939	War breaks out in Europe
1940	France falls to Germany
1941	Pearl Harbour
1942	War-time price-controls
1943	War continues, not looking good
1944	Shortage of most consumer goods
1945	Recession predicted at the end of the War
1946	The Dow hits 200, financial groupies panic that the market is "too high"
1947	Welcome to the Cold War
1948	Blockade of Berlin
1949	The USSR explodes its first atomic bomb
1950	Korean War
1951	Excess Profits Tax in the US
1952	The US government seizes steel mills
1953	The USSR explodes its first hydrogen bomb
1954	The Dow hits 300, financial groupies panic that the market is "too high"
1955	The President (Dwight D. Eisenhower) has a heart attack … and the Dow hits 400, financial groupies panic that the market is "too high"

1956 The Suez Crisis
1957 The USSR launches Sputnik
1958 Another recession ... and the Dow hits 500 anyway, so financial groupies panic that the market is "too high"
1959 Castro takes over Cuba ... and the Dow hits 600 anyway
1960 The USSR shoots down an American U-2 spy plane
1961 Up goes the Berlin Wall ... and the Dow hits 700 anyway
1962 The Cuban Missile Crisis
1963 The President (John F Kennedy) is assassinated
1964 The Gulf of Tonkin Incident ... and the Dow hits 800 anyway
1965 Civil rights protests in the USA, troops head to Vietnam ... and the Dow hits 900 anyway
1966 The Vietnam War escalates
1967 The Newark Race Riots
1968 The USS Pueblo is seized by North Korea
1969 Money tightens and markets fall
1970 War spreads to Cambodia
1971 Wage and price freeze
1972 The largest trade deficit in US history ... and the Dow hits 1,000 anyway
1973 OPEC oil price shock, the "Energy Crisis"
1974 Biggest market crash since the Great Depression
1975 Cambodia falls to the Khmer Rouge, captures Phnom Penh and the government forces surrender
1976 The world's first recorded Ebola virus epidemic breaks out in Sudan, and the Entebbe Airport crisis
1977 Tenerife Airport Disaster, the deadliest accident in aviation history

1978	Interest rates rise
1979	Oil prices keep climbing, unemployment hits double digits, Three Mile Island nuclear accident
1980	Inflation tops 14 percent in the US, interest rates at an all-time high
1981	Deep recession begins, the President is shot (Ronald Reagan)
1982	Worst recession in 40 years, the Debt Crisis
1983	Worst unemployment rate since the Great Depression ... and the Dow hits 1,200 anyway, so financial groupies panic that the market is "too high"
1984	Record US federal deficits
1985	Magnitude 8.1 earthquake strikes Mexico City, the largest city in the world. Economic growth slows ... and the Dow hits 1,500 anyway
1986	Chernobyl Level 7 nuclear disaster ... and the Dow hits 1,800 anyway, so financial groupies panic that the market is "too high"
1987	Black Monday stock market crash ... and the Dow hits 1,900 anyway
1988	Recession fears ... and the Dow hits 2,100 anyway
1989	Junk bonds collapse ... and the Dow hits 2,700 anyway
1990	Gulf War and market crash
1991	Recession ... and the Dow hits 3,100 anyway, so financial groupies panic that the market is "too high"
1992	Hurricane Andrew causes $26 billion in damages, making it the most expensive hurricane in US history.
1993	The Great Mississippi and Missouri Rivers Flood causes $15 billion in damages, and the World Trade Center is bombed.
1994	Interest rates rising

1995	The Oklahoma bombing. The Dow hits 5,000, financial groupies panic that the market is "too high"
1996	Inflation fears ... and the Dow hits 6,000 anyway, so financial groupies panic that the market is "too high"
1997	The biggest group forest fires in 200 years breaks out in Indonesia
1998	Asia Crisis
1999	Y2K fears
2000	The Dot Com crash
2001	Attack on the World Trade Center
2002	Corporate accounting scandals, the US verbal assault on the Axis of Evil, SARS epidemic
2003	War in Iraq for a second time
2004	Tsunami in Indian Ocean kills 280,000
2005	Oil and gas prices hit all-time highs
2006	Housing bubble bursts
2007	Sub-prime mortgage crisis
2008	Market crash, with the Dow's worst one-day point loss ever
2009	The US increases the War effort in Afghanistan, H1N1 flu scares people
2010	Earthquake in Haiti
2011	Fukushima Level 7 nuclear disaster, revolution in Egypt and war in Libya
2012	Hurricane Sandy causes $62 billion in damage to US Atlantic coast, Mayan Calendar 'apocalypse' fears
2013	North Korean threats of missile attacks on the US and South Korea. Boston Marathon bombings
2014	Russia appears ready to invade Ukraine and Gaza War and Ebola outbreak

In 2015, the Dow Jones Industrial Average broke through 18,000 points. And still it continues to rise. The Dow has risen through wars. The Dow has risen through chaos. The Dow has risen through recessions. The stock market shows a resilient, unstoppable forward momentum that will continue to advance through the years. It's a tough job being a pessimist. As long as the markets continue to exist, there is no bad time to invest.

Invest what you can, when you can, because the worst investment is not making one. Over the long run, the market will always rise, and if you invest wisely – based on facts, with a plan and exercising discipline – you will be better off than leaving your money to slowly erode in mutual funds or in the bank.

The market is unpredictable

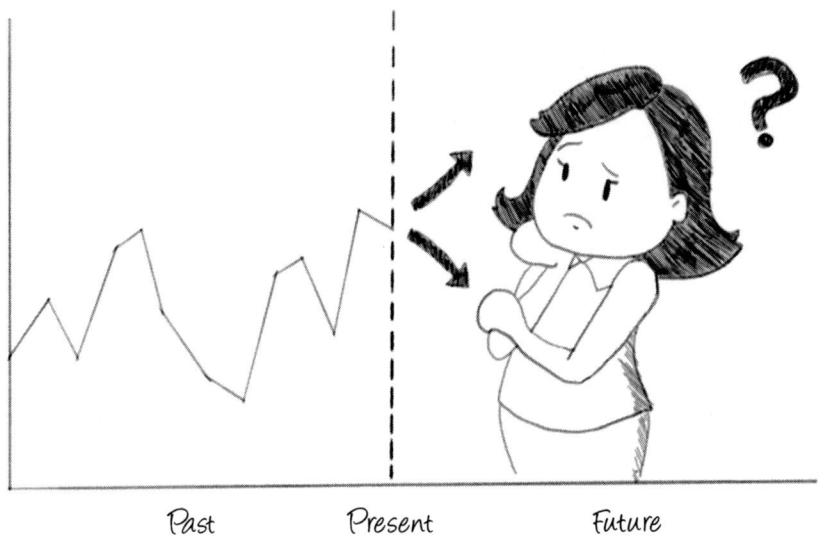

There are plenty of people who would love to tar and feather me for what I am about to tell you. So lean in close and let me whisper in your ear because I am told that I don't look good in tar and feathers.

Nobody can predict the market.

That's right. The financial experts you see on TV can't predict the market. The mutual funds managers on Wall Street can't predict the market. Madame Zenobia's crystal ball can't predict the stock market. If you don't believe me, just ask Greg Farrall, President and CEO of Farrall Wealth in Valparaiso, Indiana. He said, "There's no way to predict even with a crystal ball what the market will do today or tomorrow."

This is another universal truth.

Why would people want to tar and feather me for saying this? Because there is a lot of money in stock market predictions. There are a lot of Madame Zenobias dressed in suits and ties. In fact, there is a lot of money resting on you switching back and forth between fear and greed. Fear makes you sell at the wrong times. Greed makes you buy at the wrong times. Buy. Sell. Buy. Sell. Every time you buy or sell, somebody makes money from that transaction, and you are not that somebody.

Remember how I told you to take the emotions out? To buy and sell only on facts? To ignore hearsay and gossip, which is what market predictions are?

Remember when I told you that even the pros can't time the market, not even with their ears closer to the ground that yours or mine could ever be?

Remember how I told you to be an investor, to hold on to your stock and stick to your plan, not a trader? Investors don't pay attention to predictions. Traders live by them.

Nobody can predict the movement every time. Nobody can predict the direction with certainty. Nobody can predict the amount by a long shot. Nobody can predict the timing, not at all.

There are just too many unquantifiable factors, including politicians who speak without their brains engaged, natural disasters, bumper crops, new technologies and through it all, the unpredictable movements of human emotions.

Pundits and gurus have to look like they know what they are talking about. They make predictions. They offer explanations. The predictions are worthless. Sometimes the explanations are useful. It is worth reading what they have to say, but make sure to always separate fact from fiction.

You can't control the market

No matter how clever you are or how rich you are, you cannot control the market. A market is a meeting place where buyers buy and sellers sell. Even if you own all the stock in the world, there is no market with a buyer. It takes at least two players to make a transaction, so you could never even theoretically be in control. Very rich people and big companies can affect the market. If they go on a buying spree or dump enough stock, they can make the price go up or down briefly.

But they can't control the market.

And neither can you. You can't predict it. You can't control it. It will continue on its upward slope over time, with many ups and downs along the way. Those ups and downs are the fickle momentary emotional highs and lows people go through because they are human.

And you can't control humanity.

The market is "reasonably priced because people buy and sell a stock based on all the information that is out there. It's also fair because you can have the same information as anybody else, you just have to go out and get it," notes Ryan T. O'Donnell. Interestingly, markets are more volatile than ever, simply because we all have more access to information. More importantly, we have instant access to that information, and everybody around the world has access at the same time. This creates a global herd mentality, and the herd can change direction unexpectedly at any moment.

And with just a few clicks of the finger, we can sell or buy stock. We can react faster than once upon a time. Hey, I have a great story for you about how technology creates a crazy, silly market.

Auto manufacturer Tesla decided to pull an April Fool's joke in 2015. They announced the Tesla Model W. The headline of their press release was simply "Announcing the Tesla Model W", followed by: "Tesla today announced a whole new product line called the Model W. As many in the media predicted, it's a watch. That's what the "W" stands for."

Knowing this was April 1, recalling the fanfare over the Apple Watch, seeing the picture of a wrist with a miniature Big Ben strapped around it and knowing that an auto maker would not be announcing a watch would all be clues that this is a gag.

The markets did not think so.

The notice was posted on the company website with just five minutes left in the trading day. Within a minute, the stock had jumped by $1.50 per share to $188.50, with 400,000 shares trading. That was the heaviest trading of the stock since the first minute it was publicly listed. Over $100 million was added to Tesla's market capitalization in that one minute.

Four minutes later, at the closing bell, the stock had lost most of that instant gain.

Stock was sold. That means some people made money, and others lost. The financial news and media company, Bloomberg, suggested that some people lost as much as a few hundred thousand dollars. So what happened?

Thanks to high tech, algorithms determined that Tesla was releasing something called a Model W. Those same algorithms determined that the announcement should boost the price of Tesla's stock because a new product announcement makes a company look more successful. So many people bought stock on the assumption that they could sell it a few minutes, hours, days or weeks later to people who wanted to buy into the perceived success.

It took only a few minutes for most real humans to realize this, and the price retracted. But it was the end of the trading day, and not all the humans were paying attention.

You want to know the kicker? A couple days later, the stock began a legitimate climb, and within a couple months was passing $250 per share. Those fools who had been fooled, turned out to be fools for selling the stock they bought from a joke. Had they hung onto their stock, rather than just trading it right away, these professional traders would have made a lot of money.

You don't control the market and you cannot predict the short-term undulations in price. Look at the market from afar and accept it. Then get ready to profit from it by being a long-term investor.

So we have some universal truths. How important is the truth to an investor? In fact, all these universal truths are important because you can profit from them. Once you understand and accept universal truths, you can apply them to any stock situation.

As a challenge for the next week, I want you to look at everything that happens around you, and try to see the universal truth in the situation. This is not about investing; this is about better understanding the world around you. Investing is about the world around you, and if you can better understand things, if you can look at them in a new way, investing will make a lot more sense, too.

See you next time.

WHAT YOU LEARNED ON THIS VISIT

Money loses value.

Stocks go in only three directions.

Stock can't fall below zero.

There is no bad time to invest.

The market is unpredictable.

You can't control the market.

CHAPTER 6
Survival Tools

> *" I think every woman should have a blowtorch. "*
>
> —Julia Child

Welcome back!

So good to see you again. Come in, come in.

Let's go straight to the kitchen table, where we are going to talk about survival today. Yes, survival. Because foolish people lose their money when they go blindly throwing it into the stock market without proper survival tools. Yes, a stock can't go below zero, but going to zero is not our goal, is it?

I've already shown you how to be foolish with your money, right? Today, I will show you how to be smart. After all, survival is about staying out of danger, not flirting with it.

Best of all, Mom is back!

> *Yes, and I've prepared you some of my Home-style Chanko-nabe (pronounced chang-koh-nah-beh). This uses fresh and simple ingredients to make a very healthy dish. This is for survival.*

It's a hot pot recipe, which means it is something basic on which you can build a successful meal. So it fits very well with what we will be discussing today – survival tools on which we can build a successful investment strategy.

You see, Mom is not some hot shot financial whiz and more than a famous gastronomical hot shot. In fact, most people would probably assume she doesn't have a chance on the stock market. But she has proven them wrong, and you can, too. You need patience and discipline, but you can do it.

Investors with tunnel vision for the upside alone tread on dangerous waters. It's like going camping without having any idea on how to build a tent or start a fire, or jumping out of an airplane without knowing first how to work the parachute. It's like hiking up Mount Everest, eager to reach the top, without first planning out the supplies you'll need to get to the summit – and to get back!

The stock market is a game of survival.

Diversification

Of all the survival tools, diversification is probably the one that the most people agree upon. It is important to diversify in stocks, just as it is in your diet or in nature.

Says Ryan T. O'Donnell, CFO at The O'Donnell Group in Chico, California,"Stop worrying about individual stock returns and focus on diversification because it's the only free lunch that is out there, and we should eat as much of it as we can."

One of the really cool things about hot pot dishes is that you can throw so many different kinds of ingredients in. They are virtual incubators for diversification. So feel free to eat as much of the *Chanko-nabe* as you can.

What happens if you don't diversify your diet? Each day, you take the same nutrients in the same ratio, which means you miss out on many nutrients and numerous combinations of nutrients. You become weaker. It's a fact.

What happens if you plant a forest with only one or two types of trees. The forest becomes vulnerable to a disease. In a forest of all Elms, an Elm disease destroys the whole forest. In a forest of all Maples, a Maple disease destroys the whole forest. In Forest Gump, a Gump disease wipes them all out.

Ah, good. I see that you are listening. No, you are right, Forest Gump isn't a real forest.

Consider, however, what happens if the human gene pool is limited. If cousins marry cousins, and their children marry each other. They become "inbred". It happens in any isolated population. There just isn't enough variety in the available gene pool.

What happens if you invest in only auto parts companies, and the world suddenly makes a shift to some new means of transportation? What happens if you invest in only Russian companies and the country falls apart economically, with most of the major companies being disbanded?

Diversification in investments is critical. That means picking stock from a variety of sectors. Does that mean also investing in some mutual funds? Probably not. You want to invest in a variety of sources that are likely to beat inflation. Including a variety of coloured lolly pops in your diet is not a great way to improve your nutrition, either.

Am I saying you should invest only in stocks? Um, Mom, am I?

> *Of course not. There are a lot of good real estate investments, too. Stocks are easier to get into with limited funds to start with. Stocks require less maintenance. They don't have to be your only investment, but you can diversify across all industries by just buying stocks if you wish to.*

OK, right. Now I remember. In fact, I recall that time when we were at the supermarket and I asked you why you buy so many different stocks. You told me … do you remember what you told me?

> *I sure do, Victor. I said, "Well you see son, you see the variety of food here at this market? Think of the healthy vegetables such as broccoli, spinach, and celery as big, reliable, boring companies and those yummy chips and junk food over there as the high risk, speculative ones. And think of the stock market as the supermarket. Most people get lured into buying the tasty chips, but the vegetables here are the real foods you should buy. Every day, the prices on these vegetables change.. you don't know if their prices will be cheaper or more expensive the next day. Just like stocks. But you need to buy a variety of vegetables. You can't just eat broccoli all day long."*

Ah, yes. I don't think I would want to eat broccoli all day long. And that's when Mom started talking about salads.

> *Yes, I told you that I like to make salad by getting a variety of veggies like spinach, tomato, lettuce, cucumber, red and yellow peppers for you kids because those are healthy. Most people avoid eating veggies because they don't taste as good, but you need a good variety of them.*
>
> *I don't care to control the price, nor do I bother to predict it. The prices go up and down naturally and that's the way it is. So I usually try to buy whatever veggies are cheap, when I can. I don't try to predict or stress about when they go on sale, though. I'll buy a variety of good*

quality veggies every time I come to the market, but I pay attention to buy more of the veggies that are on sale. That way, I'm not pulling out my hair or wasting time praying that the one item I want will be at a discount!

So my point is, son, keep life simple by buying a range of healthy vegetables especially if you can get them at a discount, because that not only keeps you strong and healthy but you can save a buck or two doing it. Always buy quality, variety and at a discount. That is how I pick stocks and save money doing it."

Mom, you're getting quite chatty today.

But, you know, it's those fresh veggies that go into some of Mom's best dishes, like this *Chanko-nabe*. You need more than just one vegetable to make it, you know. Variety is not just the spice of life (and recipes), it is the essence of life (and recipes). And variety is critical to protecting your investments. On this point, almost everybody agrees.

By the way, how did that challenge go, to seek universal truths in every situation? Did you notice how important variety is? A variety of nutrients in food, as well as variety of taste. A variety of activities to keep from being bored. Did you notice that we see things better when there is a variety of colours, shades, and tones? Black on black doesn't work all that well, does it?

But variety should not mean that we load up half on stellar investments and half on weak investments that lose money over time, just as variety in a salad does not mean we load up on half vegetables and half candy.

Can you picture it – "Greek Smarties Salad"? Or "Oh Henry! Tomato Salad"? Yuck.

So it's not just variety of stocks that you need. You need a variety of strong companies.

Choosing solid companies

Mom has three simple rules for choosing the companies she invests in:

- Choose for the downside – be bullet-proof.
- Focus on solid sectors.
- Pick only the best in class.

Shall we look at these one by one?

Mom told me that most people pick stocks based on the upside. They ask themselves, "How high can this go?" That's the greed talking. I'm not saying we should not look at how high the sky can be. I am just saying that is not the best guideline for making a decision to buy.

Mom looks at the downside. She picks stocks with very little chance of going down far. She chooses bullet-proof stocks. This is a very practical approach because she does not waste large portions of her investment money on lost causes.

Actually, take a look at the math on this one. I didn't make this up; I read what Peter L. Brooks explained, "This is an obvious fact and perspective, yet most investors don't realize that if you allow a 50% loss then you need a 100% gain to get back to even."

Just imagine that you've invested $5,000 in a stock, and overnight it loses 20% value. You wake up stunned because you now have only $4,000 of stock left. But you have faith that the stock will rebound and that you will regain that $1,000 you lost. You assume that all you need is an increase of 20%. But you lost 20% of $5,000, so 20% of $4,000 isn't going to make up the difference.

I strongly believe more women can outperform men in the stock market. This is because women aren't on average as egotistical as we men are. As financial guru Suze Orman says, "Women fake orgasms and men fake finances."Women don't have the need to show off and brag to their friends to prove who's right or wrong or whose better the way men seem to.

We men always have something to prove to somebody. Face it, guys, we do, and it's this that makes us prone to making mistakes over and over. When we men get lost, we don't like to ask for directions. When a woman gets lost, the first thing she does is to ask someone. Women tend to be more practical in their approach, making them less vulnerable to failure.

My dad is a brilliant man but typical of us men. He loved buying all sorts of start up companies in hopes to "hit it big" with one shot. Sad to say that after a decade of constant news-watching, researching, trying and testing, success didn't happen.

I suggested one day that he try learning from Mom, and he turned mad like the Hulk. Aaargghh! Men don't like to ask for directions. Men don't like to be told what to do. Men don't like to follow instructions, let alone take instructions from a woman! Men like to make their own mistakes, following their own lead.

My dad didn't actually turn into the Hulk. I was just kidding. He didn't lose his cool, just his sense of orientation. The point is that his male-driven ego wouldn't care to listen. So he continues trying to prove to the family that his method is correct by exposing his money to high-risk stocks.

When soldiers walk out onto the battlefield, they understand that it takes just one bullet to end their life. It is the same on the financial battlefield. It takes just one bad stock to ruin your returns, and it often takes years to recover.

It's the same with cooking. Sure, you can try all sorts of new ingredients, but just one poisonous mushroom can make you very sick. You can protect your downside by using only safe ingredients.

So wear your financial bulletproof gear to protect yourself from the downside. As long as you don't die on the battlefield, you have a chance to survive and thrive. As Donald Trump so wisely put it, "Protect the downside, and the upside will take care of itself."

My dad was hit on the financial battlefield by a penny stock which has since been delisted on the market, and he has yet to recover from it. He is not the only one. Everybody who bought into that stock, and thousands like it, has been hit. Ouch.

Let me ask you a question. Which of the following do you think has a higher likelihood of failing? Big time-tested companies that continue to make money regardless of market setbacks, or start-up companies that are just launching?

Bingo!

By avoiding small cap companies and only buying companies that everyone depends on to live, you virtually eliminate your chances of buying a stock that fails. Of course, this increases your overall returns, since one failed stock can drag down your entire portfolio. That means buying quality companies in sectors that will be needed in good times and bad times alike protects your downside and virtually guarantees your upside.

I like how Salvatore Buscemi, Managing Director at Dandrew Partners, LLC in New York, explains the logic behind avoiding starter companies:

"A company preparing to go public can best be compared to a bride on her wedding day.

"A company is cutting expenses, a bride is sucking weight like a high school wrestler.

"A company is getting leaner generating profits, a bride is training like a Filipino boxer.

"The company uses some creative accounting to hide some losses, a bride uses layers of veneers to cover up her blemishes and imperfections.

"The company hires expensive lawyers and investment bankers, a bride purchases the best couture she can afford…

"The company will never be as highly valued, or the bride as beautiful, on their respective special day debut. Why anyone would want to buy a company so richly valued and dressed up is ridiculous on the IPO day is financial ignorance at best. I hope you'll always remember this analogy next time someone tells you about a hot IPO."

Did I tell you how important common sense is to invest successfully? Now you see why.

Did I tell you how uncommon common sense is? Ah, now you see the opportunity!

If you apply this bullet-proof approach that so many other people fail to apply, you are well on your way to making money on the stock market without the constant fear that something will go wrong. And without the competition of all those people staring at the top of Mount Everest without any thought of what to pack for dinner on the fifth day.

The first step to bullet-proofing your portfolio is to stick to critical sectors. For example, people need their cars. No matter how bad the economy is, people still need to get to work, to buy groceries and to visit each other. Even when the car companies are panicking because people are putting off their new-car purchases, people still need their cars. Investing in car parts companies is, therefore, a wise all-weather investment. Investing in car insurance companies is also a wise all-weather investment. Investing in fuel companies is a wise all-weather investment, as well. And if there have been slow sales for a couple years, it's a pretty sure bet that any surviving car company should bounce back.

Not every company in a sector represents a bullet-proof investment in that sector. For instance, a company that makes parts only for a small niche luxury car might not be the most secure. But a company that makes brakes or wipers or some other critical part for a broad cross-section of makes and models is a safe and strong investment. Brakes wear down. Wipers need replacing. If car speakers break, they can be left that way, but you just can't delay the purchase of new brake pads and windshield wipers. Those companies will still make sales, no matter how panicky people get.

It's the "make sales" part that is critical. Jacob Chapman, Managing Partner at venture capital firm Sazze Partners, explains: "Focus on the fundamentals of unit economics. How much revenue does each customer generate and how long do those customers stick around? If these numbers look good then even a company hemorrhaging money today can be a great investment."

Let's look at 12 Mom-approved sectors — and some examples:

1. **Financials – banks and insurance companies.** These companies will be around and they will always make money. Civilization would fall apart if financial systems fell apart. Banking will continue to evolve, as it has since the days when loans were issued in the temples of Babylon 4000 years ago. Banking methods might change over time, but the system itself is here to stay. And bankers will always make money.

    Death, taxes and bankers making money, right?

2. **Infrastructure – railroads, roads, port facilities, and pipelines.** You know, systems by which tangible matter is transported. As long as ships dock, oil is being pumped through the lines, and trains keep chugging along, these companies are collecting money! Pipelines is the most efficient means of moving oil over long distances and they are heavily insured against disasters, making them some of the most reliable forms of dividend payout.

But not just fuel – sugar, cattle, wheat, canola, corn, metals – anything that needs to be moved from where it is farmed or extracted to where it is processed, and anything that needs to be moved from where it is processed to where people buy it. Until somebody invents the particle transporter, this is how these things will be moved.

Have you invented a particle transporter? No? OK, just checking.

Someday we will no longer rely on oil. That day has been coming for a long time and it is still too far into the future for anybody to realistically see it.

3. **Energy and utilities – gas producers and power plants.** No matter the state of the economy, people will still need electricity and fuel. People need natural gas to warm their houses, electricity to run their computers, gasoline to run their cars – energy is critical in our daily lives. Everyone pays their utility company each month. Without energy, our civilization will come to a halt.

4. **Food – food and beverage manufactures.** Is there a more vital sector than food? You look for food as soon as you sit at my kitchen table. People won't just not buy food for a few months while the economy slumps. Just stay away from niche food companies; invest in companies that cover a wide range of basic foods that people rely on.

5. **Real estate – office towers, malls and warehouses.** This is all the real, physical, brick and mortar assets. All these physical buildings are essential to our daily lives because we live and work in them. I recommend REITs as a great way to easily invest in real estate. These are trusts that own income-producing real estate, ranging from retail space to apartment buildings, but also warehouses, hospitals, shopping centers, hotels and even timberlands.

6. **Healthcare and pharmaceuticals – drug, hospital supply, and medical diagnostic equipment manufacturers.** As long as people get sick and injured, they will need medical attention. Some healthcare companies focus on specific niches. But any that cover a broad range of afflictions is here for the long term. People might give up some entertainment, but when their health is threatened, watch how quickly they reallocate their budgets toward medicine and healthcare.

7. **Basic Materials – aluminum, steel, and chemical manufacturers.** Steel is in our cars, in our ships, in our airplanes, in our office buildings – the list goes on. Aluminum is in our machines and electronics. Chemicals are in consumer products like shampoo, makeup, and cleansers.

8. **Non-Cyclical Goods and Services – breweries, wineries, tobacco, household products, and entertainment.** Modern society uses these goods and services on a daily basis. These are also what people consume in good times and bad, and are generally not sensitive to economic conditions.

9. **Cyclical Goods and Services – apparel, advertising, hotels, restaurants, computers and electronics.** Just like non-cyclical goods and services, modern society uses cyclical goods and services on a daily basis and we will not be who we are without them.

10. **Telecommunications – *telephone*s, network providers, and *satellites* we use to exchange information.** Even the technology in your smartphone requires telecommunication services to function, right? How naked would we all feel without a smartphone nowadays?

11. **Transportation – aerospace, airlines, freight and courier, and car manufacturers.** World commerce and entire industries like tourism rest on this sector. Similar to infrastructure, this sector makes the movement of tangible objects and people possible.

12 Technology – semiconductors, software, information technology service and consulting, and hardware. Without the driving force of this sector, modern society is not possible. There will be no technological advancements in our daily lives without them, and that includes our computers and smartphones, the cars we drive, and our output efficiency.

If you get familiar with these sectors, you'll have a good idea of how to diversify your portfolio. But regardless of the sector, you want to buy only the best in class. These are the blue chip companies. Remember when I asked which was more likely to fail, start-ups or tried-and-true companies? Blue chips are the tried and true. If a recession hits and a sector is trimmed of thirty percent of its value, chances are that the start-ups will be gone, but the blue chips will weather the storm, keep making sales, keep earning income and keep passing that income along to shareholders in the form of dividends.

There might be two companies in a sector, for instance, a food processing company, with activities across multiple types of foods, and a small company specializing in a specific line of crackers. What happens when bad times hit? If the line of crackers doesn't do well, the small company is gone. The stock might well go to zero (but not below, of course). But if one line of crackers or cold cuts or preserves doesn't do well for the big company, they just stop producing that line and reallocate their resources to a line that is doing well. They don't die. They keep making profits.

A study reported in the *Journal of Financial Economics*[9] reports that penny stocks, or "over the counter" stocks, mostly perform very poorly. "Penny stocks are only appealing to the brokers who sell the penny stocks and the companies selling penny stock signals. Generally, penny stocks provide abysmal returns to the average investor (you or me)."

---

[9] The full report on the study: *http://papers.ssrn.com/sol3/papers.cfm?abstract_id=1733225*

The abstract for that study says, "… the returns on Over-The-Counter stocks are extremely negative on average. The distribution of OTC stock returns is highly positively-skewed: while many of the stocks in our sample become worthless, a few do extremely well." In other words, this is gambling, not investing. It's a lottery where a few people will strike it rich, but most people will just lose money.

If you want to gamble, there is nothing wrong with that. But why not go to Vegas or the race track and have fun gambling? Don't confuse gambling with investing.

Yes, there are some diamonds in penny stocks. But to find those diamonds requires dancing across a mine field. Not a very comforting precept.

Here is what you are investing in with penny stocks and start-ups: If this condition is just right and they get this just right and this happens, then they'll make a nice profit. But if a supplier gets some specs wrong or there are delays in arranging permits or sales projections were not realistic, the company is screwed. You don't want to invest in a company like that. As soon as there is a big "if" attached to profits, you want to look elsewhere.

Look for companies that will profit no matter what the "if" is. If the economy grows, they'll make a profit. If the economy shrinks, they'll make a profit. That's what you want in your portfolio. Make sure you really understand the companies you buy. That's why Mom invested in auto parts companies. All cars experience wear and tear and breakdown and soon require replacement parts; this is a business that makes sense to her, one that she can understand.

Here's another way to tell a good, solid, best-in-class stock from a more risky crap shoot type of stock. Ask yourself if the stock is one you could hold forever and never want to sell. If not, look elsewhere. Very often people buy a stock hoping for a quick increase in value, and then to sell it. They look to flip stock. If you see a stock as flippable material, stay away from it. That is not the type of stock for investing. Warren Buffett wisely said, "If you are not willing to own a stock for 10 years, do not even think about owning it for 10 minutes."

Mom looks for companies that are best-in-class. They have huge capitalization. They have a history of weathering storms. Try checking out how the company did during the 2008 recession and how well it came out in the following two to three years of recovery. Right Mom?

> *If you want to be paid, make sure to buy into companies that are sure to be paid. You don't need to be a math whiz. It's just common sense.*

You just have to look at the Great Depression to see what companies weathered the storm, and then came out roaring when the economy started up again. They were companies with large capitalization, in sectors that were important to society, and they had been around a long time already.

Today, that means companies like Ford and Kraft and Proctor and Gamble.

> *The purpose of choosing one stock over another is to protect your downside, and there's no better way to protect yourself than to buy only best in class companies that people like us depend on. All your companies have to do in tough times is to stay alive, and if they are best in class they should have no problem. If they are strong enough to survive a recession, one day their intrinsic value will again be recognized. So find the most resilient companies.*

Here are a few specifics to look for. This is not meant as a substitute for really studying stocks and understanding the details, but this is what a 'perfect investment' should look like according to Greg Farrall, President of Farrall Wealth in Valparaiso, Indiana:

- Completely liquid
- Complete safety
- High rate of return
- No income tax
- No skill
- High and steady dividend

Mom likes investments that are completely liquid. That's one reason for choosing blue chip stocks. They have a high trade volume. There is always activity. She can always find a buyer. Blue chips also offer complete safety having weathered all types of storms.

Mom also goes for a high rate of return, because she is in this to make money. That's why she seeks out "forever" companies. She checks the firm's projected growth. She asks questions like, "Are they in a growing or shrinking sector?" and "Do they have plans that will position them for growth within the sector?" and "What is their history of earnings?" She checks to see if they have been growing over time, and whether during bad times their growth has been more or less than average for their sector.

Remember how we talked about TFSAs? Those are tax shelters to help reduce income tax requirements.

As for "no skill", Mom is just fine with that. She likes things simple and easy to understand.

We'll talk about dividends in a moment, but if the company has kept paying dividends without any skipped or discounted intervals, that is a very powerful sign that it weathers storms easily. Even better if dividends have consistently grown. Another good indicator to check out is the cash flow. You can't pay dividends without cash.

Find good dividends

You might have noticed me mentioning dividends quite a bit over the past few minutes. Let's consider this.

Do you remember, way back when we first started talking about the stock market, why I said many investors did quite well during the Great Depression? Do you remember why they didn't get hurt by falling stock prices?

One of the reasons was because of dividends.

What is a dividend? A dividend is your share of the profits of a company. It's that simple. You can buy stock in a company because you think the company will go up in value, and you can sell your share for more later. Or you can buy stock in a company because you want a share of its profits.

These are two different goals. Of course, any sane person wants both, but dividends are more reliable generally than possible increases in value, so dividends make a great basis for buying.

> *I buy only dividend-paying stock. In the short term, who cares how the stock price goes up or down or sideways because I'm getting paid either way.*

That's just what you taught me, Mom.

Mom told me to never underestimate the power of dividends. If I put $10,000 into a stock and it pays 5% dividends annually, I'll be getting $500 every year while I am holding onto the stock. I don't have to sell any stock to make this profit.

In fact, John D. Rockefeller, said, "Do you know, the only thing that gives me pleasure? It's to see my dividends coming in." He also happens to be one of the wealthiest people to have ever lived.

Whether the company pays you on a monthly, quarterly, or annual basis, the return is easily calculable and best of all, it happens automatically. You don't have to sell, you don't even have to watch. It just happens. In fact, as a boy, this was the concept that sparked my interest in investing in the first place! I mean, how cool is that? It's like having your own small team of people working for you around the clock, non-stop, 24/7 just to pay you.

What if a stock pays out 3 percent dividends per year? Is that enough? Well, think back a couple visits ago when we had a little chat about inflation. Do you recall me mentioning that over the past century, the average inflation rate was 3.18 percent? For the past 100 years, on average, money lost value at a rate of 3.18 percent per year. In other words, a dividend of 3.18 percent is just enough to stand still. At 3 percent, you are actually losing money. Of course, if your stock is gaining in value, then you'll still be making money. But that is just something to keep in mind.

Here's another reason to love dividends. Dividend stocks tend to outperform other stocks. Why? Because companies start paying dividends only once they reach solid ground, marking up regular profits. Those are the types of companies you want to own, not the penny stocks that are much, much more speculative.

There is another reason why dividends are a smart way to determine the value of the stock. Lots of companies use creative accounting methods, with deferrals and mark-downs and other cute terms that only a creative accountant can understand (and then only after the sixth drink!). Accountants can cook the books.

They can't cook the dividends. Leave the cooking to Mom!

Accountants can hide a company's weakness behind slights of hand on the books, but they can't fake the dividends. Dividends give you a pretty good sense of the profits and the cash flow of a company. The more regular the dividends, the more solid the company, and if the dividends are substantial (more than just one or two percent, for example) and have been paid out regular as clockwork, that shows the company is both profitable and reliable.

You might recall earlier, when we were talking about real estate, I had recommended REITs. These are similar to dividend stocks because they also produce income in the form of rents for retail space, office space and so on. So no matter what the real estate market is like – hot, cold or lukewarm – you are still earning income.

The other major benefit to dividend stocks is that they give you "house money" – fresh cash that you can reinvest in more stock. So you can immediately start expanding your holdings. For me, that's just what I wanted to do. Just getting the dividend wasn't enough. I wanted something to supercharge my returns on the very stock I chose without having to make more effort! So I chose a dividend reinvestment plan, within my TFSA (tax-free savings account).

You have probably seen charts like this before…

The Power of Compound Interest

	Emily			Ethan	
Age	Portfolio Contribution	Market Value	Age	Porfolio Contribution	Market Value
25	$4,000.00	$4,320.00	25		
26	$4,000.00	$8,986.00	26		
27	$4,000.00	$14,024.00	27		
28	$4,000.00	$19,466.00	28		
29	$4,000.00	$23,344.00	29		
30	$4,000.00	$31,691.00	30		
31	$4,000.00	$38,547.00	31		
32	$4,000.00	$45,590.00	32		
33	$4,000.00	$53,946.00	33		
34	$4,000.00	$62,582.00	34		
35	$4,000.00	$71,909.00	35		
36	$4,000.00	$81,981.00	36		

	Emily			Ethan	
Age	Portfolio Contribution	Market Value	Age	Porfolio Contribution	Market Value
37		$88,539.00	37	$4,000.00	$4,320.00
38		$95,623.00	38	$4,000.00	$8,986.00
39		$103,272.00	39	$4,000.00	$14,024.00
40		$111,534.00	40	$4,000.00	$19,466.00
41		$120,457.00	41	$4,000.00	$25,344.00
42		$130,094.00	42	$4,000.00	$31,691.00
43		$140,501.00	43	$4,000.00	$38,547.00
44		$151,741.00	44	$4,000.00	$45,590.00
45		$163,880.00	45	$4,000.00	$53,946.00
46		$176,991.00	46	$4,000.00	$62,582.00
47		$191,150.00	47	$4,000.00	$71,909.00
48		$206,442.00	48	$4,000.00	$81,981.00
49		$222,957.00	49	$4,000.00	$92,860.00
50		$240,794.00	50	$4,000.00	$104,608.00
51		$260,058.00	51	$4,000.00	$117,297.00
52		$280,862.00	52	$4,000.00	$131,001.00
53		$303,331.00	53	$4,000.00	$145,801.00
54		$327,598.00	54	$4,000.00	$161,785.00
55		$353,805.00	55	$4,000.00	$179,048.00
56		$382,110.00	56	$4,000.00	$197,692.00
57		$412,679.00	57	$4,000.00	$217,827.00
58		$445,696.00	58	$4,000.00	$239,573.00
59		$481,348.00	59	$4,000.00	$263,059.00
60		$519,856.00	60	$4,000.00	$288,424.00
61		$561,856.00	61	$4,000.00	$315,818.00
62		$606,360.00	62	$4,000.00	$345,403.00
63		$654,869.00	63	$4,000.00	$377,355.00
64		$707,259.00	64	$4,000.00	$411,864.00
65		$763,840.00	65	$4,000.00	$449,133.00
66		$824,947.00	66	$4,000.00	$489,383.00
67		$890,942.00	67	$4,000.00	$532,854.00
68		$962,218.00	68	$4,000.00	$579,802.00
69		$1,039,195.00	69	$4,000.00	$630,507.00

Results

		Market Value at Age 69	# of Years Contributed
Emily	$48,000.00 Invested	$1,039,195.00	12 Years
Ethan	$132,000.00 Invested	$630,507.00	33 Years

The chart illustrates two investors, Emily and Ethan, each earn 8% return per annum. While each have an annual portfolio contribution of $4000, Emily invested $48,000 in a 12 year period from age 25 to 36 while Ethan invested $132,000 in a 33 year period from age 37. However, when it is time for them both to retire at age 69, Emily will have 40% more money than Ethan!

It shows just how much your money can grow if you leave it in an account and reinvest the interest. How does this apply to you? Very simple:

1 Invest early.
2 Buy dividend stocks.
3 Collect the dividends.
4 Reinvest the dividends in more stock.
5 Don't sell everything, stay invested.
6 Stay disciplined to your strategy.

This is how to harness the power of compound interest on the stock market.

Play with house money

"House money" is actually a casino term. Here is how it works. The "House" is the casino. Say, you play Blackjack with $100 from your own pocket. An hour later, you're up $50, and so the total you now have is $150. To play with the house's money means you put your original $100 back in your pocket and just play with the $50 you already won from the "House".

> *I like playing with the house money because once I pocket my original amount, I've removed all my risk completely from the game; whatever happens afterwards is all gravy.*

Theoretically, there's no risk involved, because even if Mom loses her $50, it's just her winnings she loses. She still has her original $100 safe in her pocket.

So here's Mom's house money recipe. I know, it's not as tasty as her recipe for Chanko-nabe or Lo Mai Chi, but it has proven to be profitable.

1 Get the first batch of house money

The same with investing, you can minimize your risk by maximizing the usage of your winnings. Say you have $1000 in a stock and the value of it climbs to $1300. Once you pull out your initial $1000, what remains is house money, in this case, $300.

2 Let the house's money sit and grow.
3 With the $1000, invest in another company.
4 The value of that stock grows to $1200. Pull out the $1000.
5 Repeat steps 2-4.

After following these steps a few times, you will own stock in several companies, Stock A, Stock B, and Stock C, all for the same $1000. Take note that house money is any amount you gain on the initial money you put in – it doesn't matter how much or how little. It might be $100 on one stock and $1500 on another. That's fine. It can be a challenge to play solely on house money, but that's the goal you should aim for. The point is to remove your initial capital completely so you can make use of that same money as a seed investment again and again. Here, have a look:

SURVIVAL TOOLS | 137

Concept of Using House Money

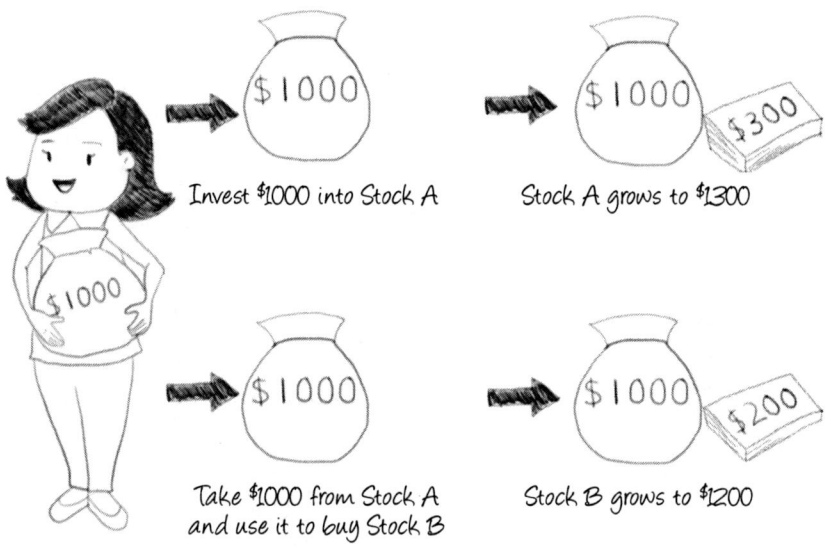

Invest $1000 into Stock A

Stock A grows to $1300

Take $1000 from Stock A and use it to buy Stock B

Stock B grows to $1200

Take $1000 from Stock B and buy Stock C

Invest $1000 into Stock C

Stock A

Stock B

Stock C

Here, I'll sketch out how this principle again but with stock growth included:

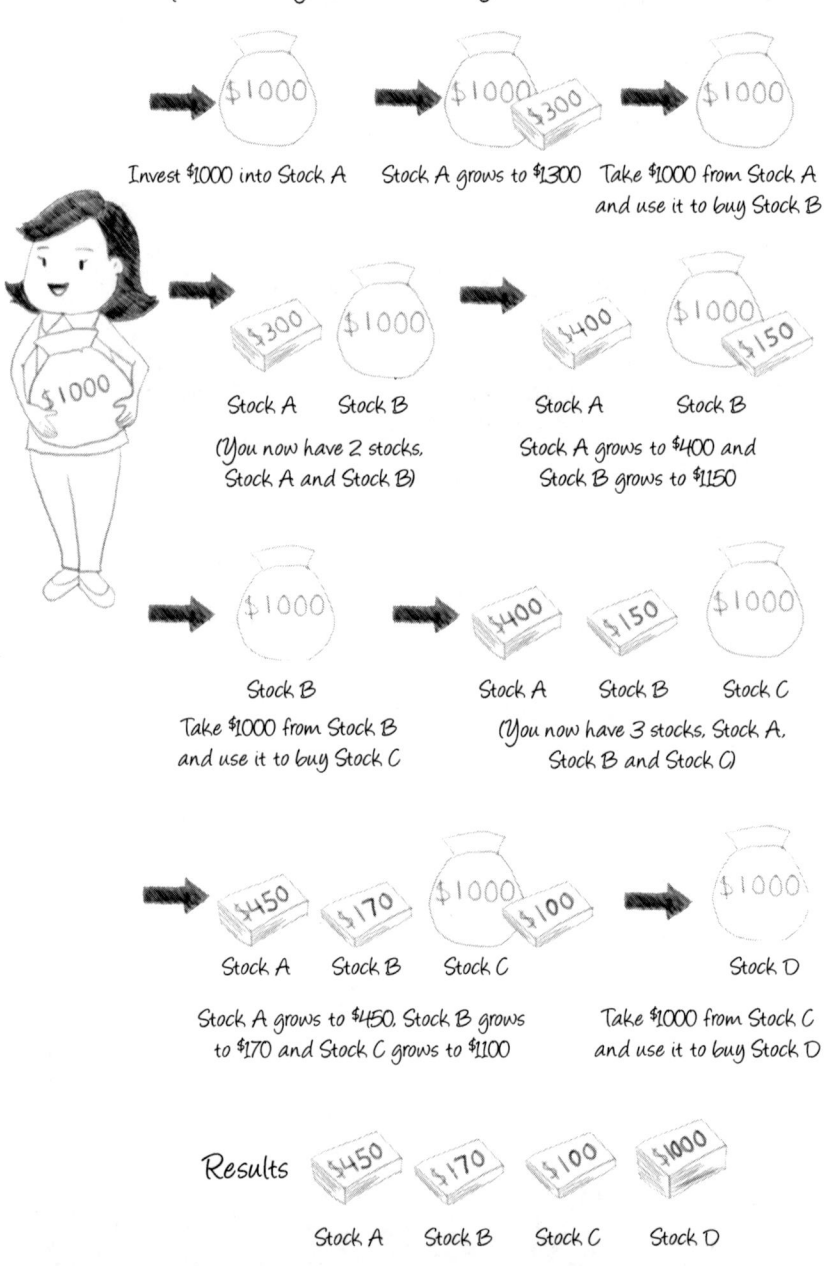

Entry/Exit Plan

Set an entry plan and an exit plan. Don't buy stock for more than you think it is worth. There are plenty of stocks to choose from. Choose the ones that are the best value for your money. If a stock is overheated at the moment, buy something else in the meantime.

Before buying a stock have an exit plan. An exit plan would be, "When this stock reaches $120 per share any time in the next three years, I will sell. Don't sell for less, even if it is plunging and everybody panics. Don't wait for it to climb higher because you already decided how high to let it go when you were detached and could exercise good judgment. When a stock seems to be on a roll toward the sky, most people lose their discipline and buy more, instead of selling while it is still high. Or they wait, hoping for it to keep climbing, which it might do ... or it might drop back.

Make a plan.

Stick to it.

No regrets.

I think I've said enough about the value of discipline last time, so onto the final survival skill, where I will share a real life example where Mom's discipline saved her from losing a lot of money.

Watch the real world

Back in 2011, Mom noticed everyone in public seemed to be carrying Coach bags. Around every corner, in every shopping mall, at every grocery store she entered, they were everywhere! Women notice these things, which men probably just ignore.

> *I go to the mall to walk around for my exercise. An hour a day. With this knee, I can't play tennis or jog, but I can walk around the mall. So I notice a few things.*

Mom notices a lot. So she went home and ordered Coach stock at about $50 per share. She knew she had done well within just a few weeks when the stock started climbing. It wasn't long before she sold her shares at around $70.

> *And used some of the profits to buy my own Coach bag!*

Exactly, because that's what we want money for – to buy the things we like.

You look puzzled. Oh, you are wondering why Mom sold her stock when it was on a tear?

> *That's one of my core principles. It's to not be greedy. When I choose my exit price for a stock, that doesn't change.*

Let's take a look at what happened with the stock. Mom bought it in 2011 for just over $50 per share and sold a year later for $70 per share, which is a 40% profit. Not bad. I'm rounding, so it was just a little less than that, but still pretty good by any standard. The stock then climbed as high as $78, then fell back below $70 after four months and into the $50-$60 range for a year and a half, and by 2014 was in the $30-$40 range.

Mom sold at around $70 because it was moving up sharply. Most people get greedy at that point and their tongues hang out and the floor gets messy with drool. Not a pretty sight. In short, they lose their discipline.

When stocks behave like that, Mom takes her money and moves on. Yes, if she could have perfectly timed her sale, she could have earned another $8 per share. But we've already established how foolish that is to try. Most other shareholders probably did hang onto their stock, hoping it would go higher still. But given the sharp decline shortly after Mom sold her shares, Mom probably did better than 90 percent of them, who chased the price down trying to hang on to as much stored value as possible and still sell before it fell even further. Yes, including professional financial advisors.

Observing what consumers are doing is a great way to pick stocks, at least for the near term. When the iPods came out a number of years ago, you couldn't walk around the mall without seeing someone listening to their white music device. Look at how Apple's stock has climbed over the years. And it's a dividend paying stock, too, so probably a good long-term investment.

> *Starbucks is another great example of a stock I read on the street. Lineups everywhere. New stores opening on every corner. Those are pretty good buy signals. Noticing those signals, I knew it was going to be a huge success, but I missed out on the action because my money was elsewhere. That's OK because it was working hard for me.*

My, look at how time flies while your money is working hard for you. Our session is over and it's time to move on to the rest of our day.

Before you go ... yes, you guessed it! Another challenge. Take some time to watch people in the mall, at your workplace, wherever. What products are they using that you have not noticed them using before? In other words, what are the up-and-coming companies whose stocks are about to improve?

I'll be interested to see your list at our next meeting.

WHAT YOU LEARNED ON THIS VISIT

The importance of diversification.

How to choose a solid company.

Find good dividends.

Play with house money.

Have an entry and exit plan.

Watch the real world.

CHAPTER 7
The Media Is Your Enemy

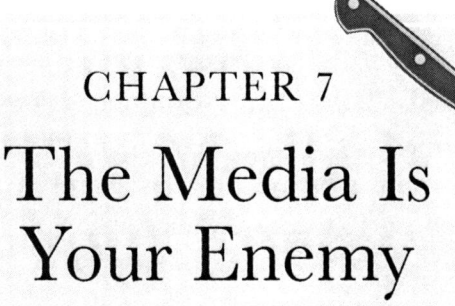

> *The average investor doesn't know where he is going, doesn't know where he's been, and is motivated only by a dim hope that if he keeps moving blindly around the arena, he'll stumble upon success. Only this never occurs because he never realizes he's a puppet and that unseen strings propel his enthusiasm ... his decisions, his stock selections, his every move. His timing is in fact, controlled by others.*
>
> —Robert Lichello

So glad you could come again. Our little chats are getting to be a lot of fun, right?

Have a seat. Say Hi to Mom.

Welcome back to our humble kitchen.

Thanks, Mom. Today, we'll talk about current events. That means, whatever is in the news. Have you ever noticed how news reports are usually filled with "bad" news?

Here a war. There a flood. Here corruption. There a murder. Here a protest. There a kidnapping. Here an oil spill. There a scandal. It just doesn't get any worse. That is our world as portrayed by the media, so I suppose it's what we want to hear.

> *I always tell Victor that CNN stands for "constantly negative news". I think it's starting to sink in.*

But the news is toxic. It's toxic to our happiness and well-being, and it is toxic to our finances. Just like these mini chocolate truffle cakes. They look so delicious. They taste so delicious. But – hands off!!! Before you reach out and take one of these, let me tell you about the ingredients. Here is what each of these contains:

- 1600 calories
- 50g of fat
- 1000mg of sodium
- 200g of sugar
- virtually zero vitamins and healthy nutrients

Don't take more than one, because they just are not good for you. Even one is not good for you unless you plan to walk home. Uphill all the way. Detouring through Chicago and Miami. Carrying a sofa on your back.

OK, OK, take one, but don't say I didn't warn you. However, you can't afford to take such a liberty with the media.

On the surface, you would think the media is your friend, right? After all, it reports company earnings, and that is useful information. It reports the opinions of economists. It reports on the price of oil and cotton and wheat. You would think this is all useful information.

So, are you ready to separate yourself from the pack running around blind, chasing their tails in hopes of making money by following the other lemmings off the cliff?

Good. Let's look at the information in the media.

Opinions versus facts

Mom taught me that there are two forces at play here. The first is fact versus opinion. Ah, I see you're nodding head that you recall our earlier discussions; always base investment decisions on fact, never on opinions. Who cares what respected financial advisors recommend? We have already seen how their recommendations do not translate into profits for you.

> *I always told Victor to buy stock based on the fundamentals, not on what some hot shot with an agenda says on TV or in the newspapers.*

The thing is that the media is really good – and I mean Wayne-Gretzky-goal-scoring-good at making opinion sound like fact. Let me give you a few examples.

- "Ford second quarter earnings were $835 million." That's a fact.
- "Ford second quarter earnings were $835 million, down from $945 million a year earlier." That's a fact.
- "Ford second quarter earnings were $835 million, up from $342 million a year earlier." That's a fact.
- "Ford second quarter earnings were $835 million, failing to live up to analysts' expectations." That's an opinion.
- "Ford will have to restructure to remain competitive and boost its earnings." That's an opinion.

- "Shareholders were disappointed with Ford's lackluster earnings report." That's an opinion.
- "Ford shares were trading heavily on unexpectedly weak earnings." That's an opinion.
- "Three new models scheduled to be released over the next month make Ford hopeful that earnings will improve in the third and fourth quarters." That's an opinion.
- "Ford second quarter earnings were $835 million. We go live to Detroit, where John Findley is standing by outside Ford headquarters. John, what's it like there?" "Well, Paul, the skies are overcast, and that pretty much reflects the mood here are the annual stockholder's meeting." That's an opinion. Actually, that's just chatter.

OK, let's take a moment to review each of those facts and opinions. Do you notice that each statement above is based on fact? Yes, technically it's all news. And if you are sitting in front of your TV, you'll accept it all as news. I mean, it is all about what's happening, so that makes it news, right? But does that make it fact?

Consider these two reports:

- "Ford second quarter earnings were $835 million, down from $945 million a year earlier." That's a fact.
- "Ford second quarter earnings were $835 million, up from $342 million a year earlier." That's a fact.

Both are technically fact, but one is bad news and the other is good news. One makes you feel like buying stock and the other makes you feel like selling stock. But the decision to buy or sell stock should be made on basic fundamentals we have already discussed. Is this a solid company? Is it here for the long haul? Does it make products people will want and need in good times and bad? Does it pay dividends regularly and reliably? Never mind what it is up from or down from, is $835 million a profit that can sustain the current level of dividends?

The facts are the same in both statements. The fundamentals are the same. Yet one report would make you buy, while the other would make you sell. This is why we must ignore the news.

And yet, the media makes all its chatter and opinion reports sound like facts. The media is a clever ol' fox. As Salvatore Buscemi says, "Be cynical at best, paranoid at worst."

Advertising is the same. If there were ads on TV for these mini chocolate truffle cakes, they would say how yummy they are, and the images would make them look delicious. They would not mention the 1600 calories or the fat and salt they pour in. They would not let you know that you really should not be eating many or even any of them.

What? No, you may certainly NOT have another.

Mom! Please come and take these away! Before we eat anymore.

Temporary versus permanent change

The other force Mom taught me to look at is long term versus short term news. Remember how we talked about the importance of having a plan and sticking to it? Don't buy and sell on a whim; buy or sell when the stock reaches the price you set to buy or sell?

Well, most of the news is short term. Quarterly earnings are not important unless they form part of a multiyear trend. Buying and selling based on three models to be introduced next month makes no sense. Ford's future does not rest on those three models. It rests on all the models for sale today, all the models still under development, the team of executives and workers running the company – the "brain trust" – and the brand's reputation.

Buying and selling based on what you see in the media makes you a trader, not an investor, and we have already seen how foolish that can be. You just can't time the market well enough to profit from minute-by-minute news reports.

But check this out. Take a look at what we have access to on this laptop. Here we go … just a couple clicks and we have all the information – all the "news" – we want in an instant. You want to know the score of the cricket tournament in India? How about the new spring fashion line released by Mark Jacobs in Milan? Or troop movements in the Persian Gulf? Whatever it is, it's just a button's click away.

The same goes for the stock market. The problem with today's world is that it is filled with too many opinions and it's becoming increasingly difficult to turn off the noise. All the "news" comes at us even if we don't search for it, filling up our feeds on Twitter and Instagram and Facebook and whatever other social network we participate in.

The news is just noise. It's just chatter. It's a herd of cattle farting on your portfolio.

You could say it's all bullsh*t.

It's all just temporary, based on the whim of whatever is trending – ooh, I hate that word. People love what's "trending" on social media, and that includes far too many financial groupies. But we both know that makes for the worst possible buy and sell decisions. Social media makes short term waves sound like real news, even more so than professional news anchors do. But it's not news. It's just noise.

This laptop has a higher purpose. Queue sound effects of a heavenly choir! That purpose is to check the actual statistics on each company and make sure the fundamentals are in place. Based on that, your opinions will usually be correct, and certainly better informed than the chatter on social media.

I had the pleasure of meeting Brian Nieves, an ex-senator from the State of Missouri, at a networking seminar one time. He told me he never watches TV programs or reads the newspaper. "Have you ever wondered why they are called television 'programs'?" he asked me.

I took the bait: "Why?"

"Because that is exactly what they do – they 'program' you to think a certain way."

All the information Nieves wants he goes out and gets purposefully. He seeks it out as he needs it, rather than mindlessly allowing TV to program his thoughts and even choose the topics he should think about.

The best way to avoid the herd mentality is to turn off the news, just as the best way to avoid eating those mini chocolate truffle cakes was to remove them from the table. Out of sight, out of temptation's reach.

Herd mentality

Have you ever watched the TV show *Who Wants to be a Millionaire?* Contestants can ask the audience for help. It's called a "lifeline". And the audience is usually right because they make decisions in isolation, as individuals, not one following the other as a crowd or a herd. Show host Regis Philbin once reported that the audience is right 95 percent of the time.

However, if you listen to the stampeding herd that is reacting to media opinions, your opinions will be affected by the herd and you will get trampled by the herd. Remember, when everybody else is buying, that's usually a good time to sell. And when everybody else is selling, that's usually a good time to buy. As John D. Rockefeller once said, "The way to make money is to buy when blood is running in the streets".

So pay attention for reports of blood running in the streets. If used correctly, the media can actually be your friend.

Yeah, yeah. I know I said the media is your enemy, but that's only if you pay attention to all the farting cows. If you ignore the media and watch the crowd, the media can be your friend. For instance, let's say the media report goes something like:

"Ford second quarter earnings were $835 million. We go live to Detroit, where John Findley is standing by outside Ford headquarters. John, what's it like there?" "Well, Paul, the skies are overcast, and that pretty much reflects the mood here are the annual stockholder's meeting."

Blood is running in the streets. The farting cows do what farting cows do best. The herd sells. Stock prices dip 3.2%. You buy at a discount.

Yes, yes, you are right. It makes perfect sense. And yet, it is programmed into our DNA through thousands and thousands of years of evolution to follow the crowd, because the crowd offers protection from our enemies. Most people will seek comfort in the farting cows to protect them from getting blood on their shoes. Do not let this animal instinct ruin your financial success.

What's that? Oh, yes, that's a very good question. What if your own opinion happens to be the same as the herd's? That can happen, just as the audience on *Who Wants to Be a Millionaire?* reach the same conclusions independently. It's like that Billy Joel song: "For all our mutual experiences, our separate conclusions are the same."

Coming up with the same answer as everyone else does not make you wrong, as long as your thinking isn't influenced by everyone else talking about it. As long as your opinions are based on fact, not on chatter.

I want to encourage you to have independent thinking. Distinguish between facts and opinions. Form your own opinions based on facts, and never accept the opinions of others as fact. "Everybody has an opinion, and if you're to become a student of investing, you have to be very careful that you're not listening to every talking head,' points out Greg Farrall.

Let me ask you a personal question. You don't have to answer out loud, just think about the answer. Here's the question: have you ever been influenced by somebody else, when you really should have believed in yourself?

I'll tell you my answer. Yes.

It happened to me when I was in high school biology class. I glanced over at Jon's paper towards the end of an exam. To my surprise, the answers I saw on a section of his test were different from mine. Jon was an A student, so I was pretty sure that he was confident about his answers. So I quickly changed my answers to match his answers, just seconds before we had to hand in the papers.

Guess what happened? We got our papers back shortly after, and when I looked at the results, it turned out that the answers I had changed in the last minute were wrong. I actually got a worse mark because I regarded his opinion higher than I regarded my own.

It is soooo easy to be swayed by the media. We all say "You can't believe everything you read in the news." But we all believe it anyway. It's true! There is a whole branding process based on "As Seen On TV". Flip to the back cover of any book in the bookstore and you'll find a couple quotes from highly-regarded media.

"A thrilling read!" – *The New York Times*.

"It had me spellbound!" – *USA Today*.

Remember that people on TV can say whatever they want, because when you buy or sell stock, it's not their money on the line; it's yours. So make sure that when it's your money on the line, it's your own, independent opinion that makes the call, that you are not influenced by the noise and chatter and the stomping hoofs of the stampeding herd.

Just say no to mini chocolate truffle cakes and cattle farts!

The media in real life

Let's look at a few things that really happened. Mom, I'm going to need to borrow your laptop to show our guest a few charts. In 2008, the market crashed. We all know it. The economy tanked. As I said earlier, if you want an excuse to panic, you can always find one. Every year there are dozens of great excuses to panic.

You can panic in pairs, in groups or by yourself. Even introverts can join in. You can panic on the farm or in the city. This makes panic the ideal DIY activity.

But panic and fear are not what DIY investors like you or me should do. In 2008, when everybody was panicking, Toyota stock fell from $90.92 to $58.17 in just two months. There is a word for this: freefall. There is another word for this: Panic!

Yes, blood was running in the streets.

A lot of panicking shareholders sold their stock at $80 and at $70 and, in a panic that probably included a lot of medication, thereby boosting pharmaceutical stocks, some eventually sold at $60.

A few more level-headed people bought the stock at $80 and at $70 and at $60. How do I know this? Because no stock sells unless there is a buyer for it. So there were buyers at every price that there were sellers.

Within a year, Toyota stock had recovered most of its losses and was trading at $86.

The fools who panicked lost a lot of equity. They also probably lost a few years of their life from the stress.

The wise people who looked at the long-term fundamentals of the Toyota Motor Corporation hung onto their stock or bought more. By 2014, the stock was trading in the $130s, topping $140 for a while. So panic didn't pay off.

From a different perspective, Toyota stock was trading at $7.50 per share in the mid-1980s. So falling to $58 still meant that it had grown amazingly over three decades. Put in that light, the panic seems downright silly. We're in this for the long haul, and if you make good investments and stay invested, you'll be much wealthier and less stressed than traders trying to time the market.

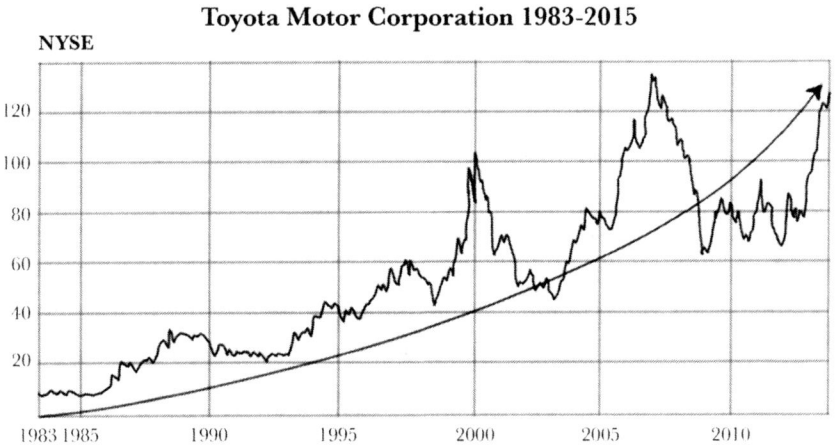

Traders listen to the cow farts. Investors draw their own conclusions. Yes, you can quote me on that!

Here's another example. Canadian National Railway Company has suffered a string of bad news. There have been crashes. There have been derailments. There have been spills.

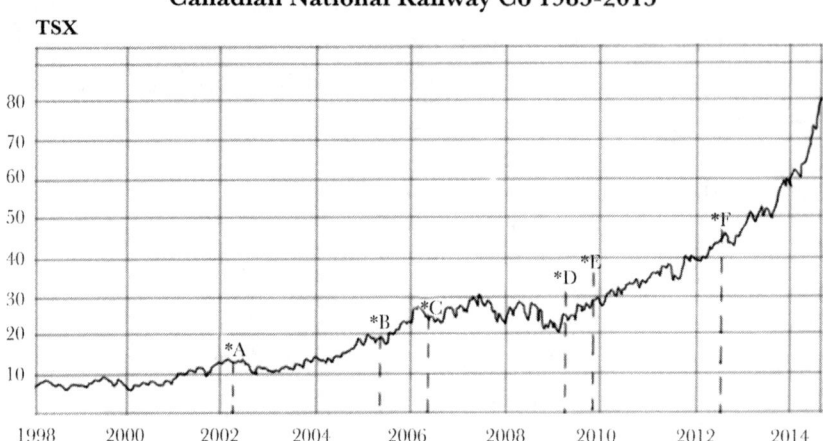

Take a look at the chart:

*A) In May 2002, CN spilled dangerous goods spilled near Firdale, Manitoba, which burned for the next three days.

*B) About 40,000 litres of caustic soda spilled into the Cheakamus River in British Columbia in August 2005 from CN trains. The fish population was decimated. That same month, 1.3 million litres of heavy bunker C fuel oil and 700,000 litres of pole treating oil spilled into Wabamun Lake in Alberta. CN was fined $1.4 million for its failure to follow federal and provincial environmental safety regulations.

*C) In June 2006, a derailment caused a spill of 233,000 litres of hydrocarbons in Quebec.

*D) In June 2009, a train derailment caused a spill and a massive explosion of ethanol in Illinois. The fish population was decimated. The courts awarded US$36 million to plaintiffs in a negligence lawsuit against CN for loss of life, injury and associated damages.

*E) In December 2009, propane, benzene, and plastic pellets were spilled near Spy Hill, Saskatchewan, igniting and burning 34 rail cars for 6 days.

*F) In November 2012, 5,700 litres of diesel fuel spilled from a CN train onto the tracks and flowed into the ecologically sensitive Squamish Estuary in British Columbia.[10]

There are examples that go back further. These are just some of the more spectacular ones in recent history. Note that many of them involve significant environmental damage and some also loss of human life. There were huge clean-up costs and in some cases, significant fines, not to mention the loss of some very expensive cargo.

My condolences to the families affected by these tragedies. I felt terrible researching this news. But it illustrates the point. Despite the derailments, the lawsuits and financial setbacks since 2002, and many others that happened before, the stock price kept rising. In May 2002, it was $6.46, and it rose steadily to $12.59 in June 2009. The stock traded as high as $83 in 2014.

If that's a stunned look on your face, no kidding. It blows my mind, too. A company can suffer disaster after disaster, at a huge cost to its own bottom line, endure lawsuits for negligence that ends up in death, and still make attractive profits for its shareholders.

Here's another example. The Goldman Sachs Group is a huge American investment banking firm.

*A) In April 2010, Goldman Sachs was charged with fraud by the SEC. It was a huge scandal in the United States. The Dow fell 126 points. Goldman Sachs stock fell below $140 per share.

*B) Then, with what some call one of the worst financial disasters to hit Europe, the European debt crisis was in full swing in 2011 through 2012. As a result, Goldman Sachs took another plunge falling to as low as $88 per share in November 2011.

---

[10] Additional incidents can be found at *http://www2.gov.bc.ca/gov/content/environment/air-land-water/spills-environmental-emergencies/spill-incidents/past-spill-incidents*

*C) A statement released to the media by the firm in December 2012 states, "Over the coming 18 months, prospects for economic activity in the euro area are bleak. Within the recently published Goldman Sachs Euro Area Outlook note, we forecast that the current recession will extend well into next year, with at best sub-trend growth envisaged for 2014."[11]

*D) By the end of 2014, with many more ups and downs in between, of course, the stock had not only recovered but was reaching $200 per share. And the stock dips were just that – dips.

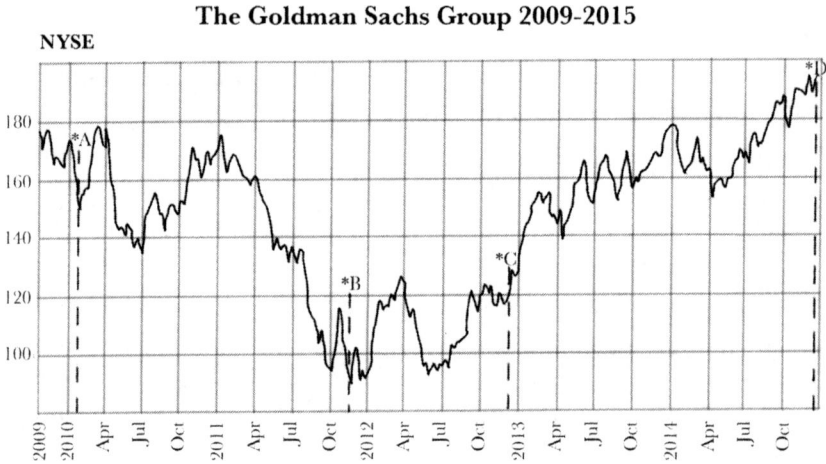

What all these examples clearly demonstrate is that while the media can run around with their hands in the air, wailing about the end of life as we know it, and everyone else can run around in general panic, life goes on. Commerce goes on. Profits go on. And your investments continue to build wealth.

In the words of business guru Timothy Ferriss, "Once you realise you can turn off the noise without the world ending, you're liberated in a way that few people ever know." Mom taught me to turn off the noise.

---

[11] http://www.goldmansachs.com/media-relations/in-the-news/archive/pill-oped-12-9-2012.html

> *I hate noise. Earning reports, income statements, facts – those are the important things. I watch the news, but I just laugh at what is mostly just gossip and speculation. Any major company will overcome momentary hardships and continue to produce extraordinary profits. It's the long run value of the stock that's important.*

I think Mom summarizes very well what we have been talking about today. Let's just add that we must stick to our plan. We talked about this before. If we don't listen to the media, what do we do? We stick to our plan. If the stock dips, we don't sell. If the stock rises, we don't sell – unless it rises to the point where we had planned to sell.

For any really significant company, you might not have a selling price. You might just want to hold the company right through to retirement because it's going to keep rising decade after decade, as we saw happening with Toyota stock. But whatever your plan, stick to it.

And buy stock when it dips. If you have a target price for buying, do so. The media is your friend if you let it make everybody else panic while you remain focused. Let them foolishly sell their stock, and you'll be there to buy it. And when the stock recovers, you'll be the one to profit.

Let me stress again that you'll profit from buying fallen stock only if the company is solid. Some companies suck. Yes, it's true. You can quote me on that, too. Some companies suck.

Some companies are here today, gone tomorrow, and the stock falls because it's almost tomorrow. And tomorrow it might be worth zero. Make sure that when you buy stock, it's for good solid companies, as we discussed last time. Companies with history. Companies with regular dividends. Companies who profit in good times and bad.

I see that the clock on the wall says that our time today is just about up, I want to leave you with one simple challenge.

I want you to ignore the media until 6:00 pm every day until we next meet. Don't turn on the radio in your car; listen to a CD instead. Don't read magazines. Avoid anything that passes for "news" on the Internet. That means stay off of social media, too. Stay away from all gossip in the office; people will just have to understand that it's an unusually busy week for you. Do this until 6:00 pm every day.

> **WHAT YOU LEARNED ON THIS VISIT**
>
> The media is your enemy.
>
> The media reports opinions that sound like facts.
>
> The media reports short-term events, not what counts over the long term.
>
> People are like cattle, following the herd — and that makes for bad investing.
>
> The media doesn't affect the long-term price of a stock.
>
> Don't listen to bullsh*t.
>
> Stick to your plan.

CHAPTER 8
Mom's Ten Commandments of Investing

"You have to learn the rules of the game. And then you have to play better than anyone else."

—Albert Einstein

Welcome back.

Hey, you are smiling. Yes, you are looking healthy and relaxed and ... say, did you follow my challenge? Have you been ignoring the media? You wear it well.

Come on in.

Mom's kitchen must feel familiar to you by now, the oak cupboards, the beige countertop, the tray of sauces in the corner of the counter, the spice rack. I don't think a thing has changed since the first time you arrived.

Well, you know what? Nothing changes today, either, because we are not really going to cover new ground. In fact, what we are going to do is to bring together all the various points we have already discussed and give you an easy-to-follow set of guidelines. These are Mom's Ten Commandments of Investing. If you follow these guidelines, even if you do nothing else, you should be able to make it.

We are boiling down Mom's recipe for investing.

But first, have a delicious *Mochiko* cupcake. I made them myself. It's got a gummy-soft chewy texture with a light sweetness that's not overpowering. Perfect for binge – snacking on. One try and you'll be hooked.

Hmmm.

Have some tea to go with it; it should be good. Oh, Mom. Love what you did with your hair, by the way.

> *Oh, I just had a trim. When your hair is short and wavy, you don't have much you can do with it.*

Ah, but you are beautiful. Simple, sensible hair in basic black. Just like your simple and sensible investing guidelines.

It's important to think of her commandments as the ingredients to have in every investing recipe, it's kind of like a hot pot or a stew. The ingredients are all thrown together and mixed about. And nothing is carved in stone. There are exceptions to every rule. Mom herself doesn't always follow her own recipe, although she is very careful to stay true to her principles which I'll now share:

Have a simple plan.

The funny thing about the stock market is that it is a vast complex institution, made up of many vast, complex institutions. Let's face it, the whole thing is pretty complicated.

Most people assume that because the stock market is complicated, so should be their investing plan. They think that if their investing plan is not complicated enough to match the market, it somehow won't work. They think that the only money to be made in stocks is through some complicated formula. The thinking goes something like this – yes, this is confusing and this is just an example of the strange type of thinking that goes into the complex-plan process:

- The more complicated the plan, the less you'll understand.
- The less you understand it, less other investors will be able to understand it.
- The less other investors understand it, the less likely they are to adopt the plan.
- The fewer investors adopt the plan, the more money it will make.
- And the more money the plan makes, the richer you'll become.

To that, I say "Poodle drool!"

Sure, I know some more colourful language than that, but let's just stick with "Poodle drool!" for now.

Mom always told me to keep things simple. She told me that if a plan starts to be complex enough that it could become confusing, it's already too complex. You need to really understand your plan and be able to follow it without having to over think it. The simpler the mechanics of your plan, the less that can go wrong.

I like how Peter Lynch put it: "Never invest in any idea you can't illustrate with a crayon."

Mom also told me to stick to my plan, no matter what. Tweak it. Improve it. Make it more efficient. But don't change it. Ninety percent of people fail to profit from the stock market because they don't have a plan or they fail to follow their plan. Patience is virtue – devise a simple plan and put it in writing. Then follow it and keep following it.

Diversify

I know its cliché but don't put all your eggs in one basket. Buy stocks in various sectors. You know what sectors to pick, and you know what kind of best-in-class companies to buy in each sector. Just make sure to cover a wide variety of stocks.

Don't just invest in Canada or in the USA. Invest in other safe countries.

But don't just invest in stocks. Invest in other solid investments. Real estate is solid, so that is also a good bet, especially rental properties that keep drawing rent (like stocks that earn dividends). Again, within real estate, it is best to diversify. Pick different cities. Pick both commercial and residential.

Just as Mom keeps a variety of spices on the spice rack in the corner, variety is the spice of investing, too.

In fact, it's more than just about spices and it's more than just about taste. It's about basic health. Consider the fruits and vegetables and meats you eat. It is very important to get variety in these, because it is important to get a variety of vitamins, minerals and other nutrients.

Vitamin A is very healthy for you, so carrots are a good food to eat. But you also need other nutrients. Adding sweet potatoes and liver to your diet can help, but they are also vitamin A rich foods. Yes, they are good, but they do not replace lettuce and bananas and fish and blueberries and peas.

> *I am always looking to balance out the various kinds of foods when I shop. Variety is important.*

Variety is important for your stock portfolio, too. If you own two bank stocks, buying two more won't diversify your portfolio. You should also add some infrastructure stocks and some food stocks and some transportation stocks. Balance is important.

Never borrow to play

If you have been paying attention to Mom's recipe, you might have noticed that she never took out a loan to buy stocks. She saved up to buy her first stocks. After that, she played with house money. House money is that same initial money she invested in those first stocks.

Let's revisit how that works.

First, you buy stocks with the money you have. Those stocks increase in value. When they increase enough, you can sell some of the stock to take out the original investment. What is left is the house money, which you keep in play. You can use the original amount again to buy another stock.

If the stock rises enough that it hits the "sell" mark in your plan, you can sell the whole lot and take a profit. Remember that's what Mom did with Coach stock? In that case, it's all house money, so go ahead and invest as much of it as you want in new stocks.

And then there are the dividends collected along the way, which are pure profit. You can reinvest those in whatever stock you want to buy next, or you can spend the money as you wish. Only spend this dividend portion, though, never your principle.

Just don't borrow money. Why am I so picky on this point? Simple — borrowed money is money you cannot afford to lose. You owe it to somebody. Borrowing money to buy stocks is a form of gambling, and gambling is not investing.

Never invest money you cannot afford to lose, because no matter how sure a stock is, there is always the possibility that it will go to zero. Remember Nortel? Yes, that was a once-in-a-lifetime catastrophe, but lightning can strike again.

Mom has seen people lose their homes and forced to sell their businesses to pay others back because they were playing on borrowed money.

There are some people who advise borrowing to invest. They say you can leverage the borrowed money to make a much bigger profit, much faster. Borrowed money does provide leverage, which can be a good thing, but it also increases your risk monumentally, especially if one of your stocks does go to zero. Your own money going to zero is one thing. Zero is as low as the stock can go. But if you borrow to buy the stock, it can go much lower because a debt not paid off keeps growing and growing.

Own as many stocks as possible (on house money)

This is a growth commandment. When you first buy stocks, you will probably select just one company, or perhaps a handful of companies, depending on how much money you have saved for investing. But as you start to profit, you'll be able to free up house money and you'll collect dividends.

It is worth revisiting the theory Mom uses to build and expand her portfolio:

1. Buy Stock A.
2. Stock A price rises > sell some Stock A
3. Use Stock A proceeds to buy Stock B
4. Stock B rises > sell some Stock B
5. Use proceeds to buy stock C
6. Stock C rises > sell some Stock C

Where should you invest those available funds? Don't put them back into the same stock. Don't put them into the same sector. Did you notice how Mom invested in a new sector with each wave of investments? That approach allowed her to use a fairly limited initial investment, the house money, to diversify her portfolio. But if she was to do it over again, the Stock A and Stock B and Stock C would all be in different sectors, to spread the risk and to spread the opportunity.

This rule combines the rule to diversify and to always play with house money. Of course, it stands to reason that the companies should be solid investments. Don't keep diversifying if it means compromising quality. Stick to companies that are solid and will be there for the long term, dividend-producing companies that create real value that people cannot live without in good times and bad.

It's a numbers game

Remember that investing is a numbers game. You put a certain amount in. You earn a certain profit. You take a certain amount out.

There can be a lot of emotion in investing, especially greed and fear. We have already seen that. Greed makes us view shaky investments as a sure thing. We ride the wave of wishful thinking, of wanting to believe that this time we'll hit the jackpot. As Sir John Templeton said, "The four most dangerous words in investing are: 'This time it's different.'"

Ignore those destructive wishful thinking impulses. Ignore your inner greed. It won't be different.

Fear makes us view solid investments as risky. We hear bad news and fear that the whole house of cards will come tumbling down. We sell solid stocks, just because there is a little extra breeze in the air.

Ignore those destructive panic impulses. Ignore your inner fear.

Base your decisions on sound data. Is the company well-capitalized? Is the company established? Has the company proven its staying power? Does the company continue to pay steady and reliable dividends through good times and bad? Is its price to earnings ratio good for its sector? Does it provide a product or service that people need, no matter what?

Focus on the facts, and those facts are mostly numbers. You don't need to be a math whiz, by the way. Mom's not a math whiz.

> *Not at all. I can count and I have a calculator to figure out a few simple ratios, but it's not really about doing math. It's just about comparing numbers.*

And more importantly, Mom, it's about being able to separate the pure numbers from the idle speculation, fact from fiction.

Stay invested

This is where *The Hitchhikers Guide to the Galaxy* comes in handy. Don't panic.

And don't trade.

What you want is to have your money staying as long as is useful in a stock. You don't want to keep trading back and forth because we have already seen how investors usually win and traders usually lose.

Stay invested in a stock until it hits the price you had set and planned to sell.

But staying invested is more than just holding onto stock for more than a year. It also means that when you do sell, you should not keep the cash sitting around your house or in your bank account too long. You should watch for another solid company to invest in, ideally getting stock at a nice price when there is a small dip.

While money sits in your drawer, it doesn't make new money for you. When it is invested, at the very least it is making you dividends. And you don't want to miss out on earnings. So you want to keep your money in stocks as long as possible.

Be a contrarian

Warren Buffett said it best, "Be Fearful When Others Are Greedy and Greedy When Others Are Fearful."

I know I told you to keep emotions out of this. I don't really mean that you should be fearful or greedy, just that you should act that way when others are being greedy or fearful. You can, without getting caught up in emotions, take advantage of how others foolishly get caught up in their emotions.

In any situation where price is determined by supply and demand, you want to be contrarian. When people are rushing to sell, be helpful by buying from them. When people are rushing to buy, be helpful and sell to them. It pays to be helpful. It's not just good karma; it's common sense. You want to be the one in short supply, whether that is being a buyer or a seller, because that pushes up your value.

Remember that it's a numbers game. So when you see that people are starting to sell a stock you've been watching, don't buy too early or too late. Wait for it to come down to the price you are planning to buy it at. Then buy.

The same goes when people are buying up a stock you own. Wait until the stock reaches the price you planned to sell it at. Then sell.

In both situations, you need to have a plan. That was the first commandment we visited when you first sat down at this table today. Don't forget to have a plan, because if you don't, all you'll have to fall back on is ... no, I can't say it ... emotions!

Victor. I rarely see you so emotional!

Please, Mom. Not now.

Don't be a trader

Do I sound like a broken record? If there is one piece of advice that I think I have given you most often, probably because it is linked to so many other facets of investing, it is "Don't be a trader." I am sure you would be scratching your head if I left this one out of Mom's Ten Commandments of Investing.

In theory, you would ideally like to buy once and never have to sell. The fewer transactions you make, the less profits leak from your portfolio into transaction fees and such. But you do sometimes have to sell, and you certainly do want to buy more than once, if for no other reason to invest your dividends. So your goal should be to minimize selling, to sell only with a specific purpose. And buying should have just as much purpose, based of course strictly on the numbers.

Always keep cash on hand

OK, so you noticed. Yes, this seems it contradicts what I said earlier about staying invested. I know that I said, "While money sits in your drawer, it doesn't make new money for you. When it is invested, at the very least it is making you dividends." And that is true.

But it is also true that if you don't have cash on hand, there is no opportunity to buy new stocks. You need to have that house money or cash available to buy new stocks.

It reminds me of the story of the ant and the grasshopper. The ant worked hard, robbing picnics and storing food away, always having a cache in case some unforeseen event might occur. The grasshopper chided the ant, "Why you work so hard, ant? Relax. Life's a picnic. Enjoy it."

But one day, winter came along – something that caught both the ant and the grasshopper off guard because, well, they are insects, right? They don't live long enough to understand about seasons. The ant bunkered down with his cache of food, while the grasshopper starved to death.

The moral of the story is that ants like picnics more than grasshoppers do.

No, wait, that can't be right. The moral of the story is to always have a reserve.

"In 2008 for example, anyone who was fully invested in mutual funds lost roughly 40% of their funds," notes David Bickerton. "Some mutual funds may have gone down 39%, some 41%, but anyone invested in the broad market was punished for being fully invested. This issue really speaks to the value of holding cash for buying opportunity in difficult times."

We are dealing with a balancing game here. The whole point of keeping cash on hand is so that you'll have buying power when a stock you are watching dips to the level you set to buy it at. The only reason to keep cash on hand is so that you can use it and no longer have it on hand. The ant didn't just store his food away; he ate some of it as he went.

So, yes, it's an oxymoron. But isn't that the whole idea behind having money. We work so hard to get more and more money, but the only use we have for it is to give it away.

So don't get too caught up in this commandment, but also don't rush to buy back into a stock. Take your time and make sure you are getting a good deal according to your plan. You don't want to buy any old stock just because it's available, then two months later be short on cash when a stock you really want becomes available.

Be patient

Is this the hardest commandment of all, or what?

> *This is definitely the hardest one for Victor. Watching the stock market do its roller coaster ride, just sitting there watching, not doing anything. Victor finds that hard.*

Right you are, Mom. I think most men find that harder than women do. We see things happening and we feel we need to act, to take control of the situation.

Of course, it's just an illusion. We can't take control. The only thing we can do is buy or sell. And we should never buy or sell just to say we are doing something. After all, our goal should be to avoid selling unless absolutely necessary, and to sell only when the right opportunity presents itself. Every action we take must have a purpose.

It's just like what Adrian Chan, my uncle, and mentor asked me while we were having dinner at a local Boston Pizza one night, "Victor, do you know the difference between speed and velocity?" Although I remember having the urge to quote Top Gun, it was better at that moment to let him reveal his point. "The difference is that speed lacks direction. You can run around in a circle really, really fast and you will have lots of speed, but you end up going nowhere. Spending energy going around in circles isn't efficient either, so in life along with everything you do, be efficient and have velocity."

To have velocity is to buy and sell without being wishy-washy. To be efficient is doing it only when the right opportunity presents itself.

Acting just to feel like we are doing something makes no sense. But for a lot of us, especially for us guys, it's hard to sit on our hands and just let the stock market take its course. This is where I said that women have an advantage in the stock market.

The thing is, and this is the crazy thing, if you are in it for the long run, why do you want to act right away? Your money is in it for the long run, right? So let your money do its work. Give your money time to grow. Be patient with your money if you want it to bring home the sweets.

When you are itching to act, and you know you should be patient, that's the time to power down the laptop. Read a book. Play a video game. Sign up for salsa classes. Catch flies with chopsticks. Whatever that adds betterment to your life in other ways without mucking around in your investments, that's what you should do. And to my mentor Adrian, that's efficiency.

So there you have it: ten commandments. Now these are not like the commandments you see in drawings, carved on stone tablets. I use the word "commandments", but it's up to you to decide whether to follow them. I don't have a lightning bolt, and even if I did, I would not strike you down for disobeying any of these.

It's your money. You decide.

These are the rules by which Mom invests, and they have helped her accumulate wealth much faster than a middle-class housewife would be expected to.

Well, that's a lot to think about, and I know you're ready to get on your way.

But first, can I leave you with this quote?

"Investing is an art, and the ability to distill an investment process down to its most useful or necessary pieces is as important as having an all-star investment team." So said Jason Hilliard, President and Chief Investment Officer at Forecast Capital Management, LLC in Denver, Colorado.

Take some time to think about these commandments and what they can mean for you. We have one more session together, and we'll be getting very personal next time. So come back refreshed.

Yes, that's your challenge. Just come back refreshed.

WHAT YOU LEARNED ON THIS VISIT

Have a simple plan.

Diversify.

Never borrow to play.

Own as many stocks as possible.

It's a numbers game.

Stay invested.

Be a Contrarian.

Don't be a trader.

Always have cash on hand.

Be patient.

CHAPTER 9
An Hour in the Life of Mom

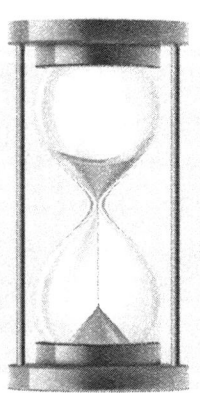

> *“Formal education will make you a living; self-education will make you a fortune.”*
>
> —Jim Rohn

Great to see you again. Come in, come in, come in.

Let's just head over to the table and take a look at what Mom is up to. Yes, that's right. I asked you to come a little early today so we can take a peek at what Mom does and how she does it – you know, a little "show and tell".

How was that last challenge? The easiest one yet, I'll bet.

We've talked a lot about theory and strategies, but have you wondered what Mom actually does with that hour she spends each day? Ah, you are looking at me questioningly, and I know what you are thinking. You are wondering why mom spends an hour per day on her stock portfolio if her strategy is to buy and hold, to ignore the daily fluctuations of the market and look at the long-term trends. Why not just review her portfolio once a month? Or even once a year? Why spend an hour every day? Mom, what do you have to say?

> *I like to keep very close tabs on my stocks. I like to know when each stock starts making a big change so that I am ready to act or even change my strategy. I won't act on the first impulse, but I will watch when stocks are making significant moves. The last minute is never a good time to make decisions about anything.*

So you see Mom is checking her current holdings to see where each of her stocks stands. This way she can tell if any of them is approaching her sell prices.

You remember how important it is to have a plan, right? How Mom always knows what price she will sell the stock? We'll take a look at a sample plan for a sample stock, but first, let's revisit her overall investing plan, the template into which any single stock plan fits:

1. Buy Stock A.
2. Stock A price rises > sell some Stock A
3. Use Stock A proceeds to buy Stock B
4. Stock B rises > sell some Stock B
5. Use proceeds to buy stock C
6. Stock C rises > sell some Stock C

So we can see that the ultimate plan when buying any stock is to sell some, not all, of that stock. This is because the more you sell some of the stock, the more you can buy into others. The more you buy into others, the more you diversify. And the more you diversify, the stronger your portfolio gets. In theory, the value of what she sells is equal to the value she put in, before profiting from growth and dividends.

So let's look now at what a plan for buying and selling an individual, hypothetical stock might look like…

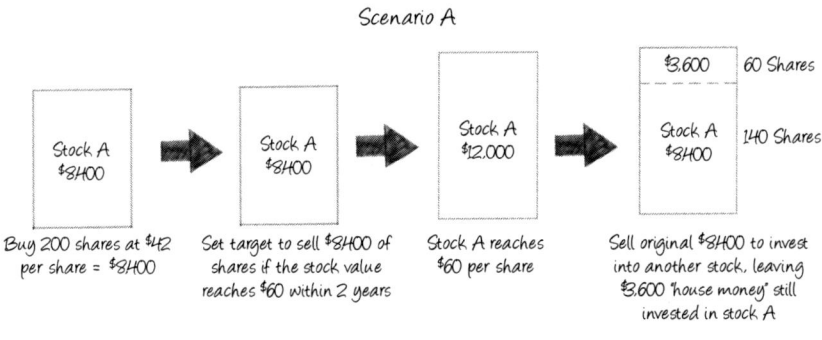

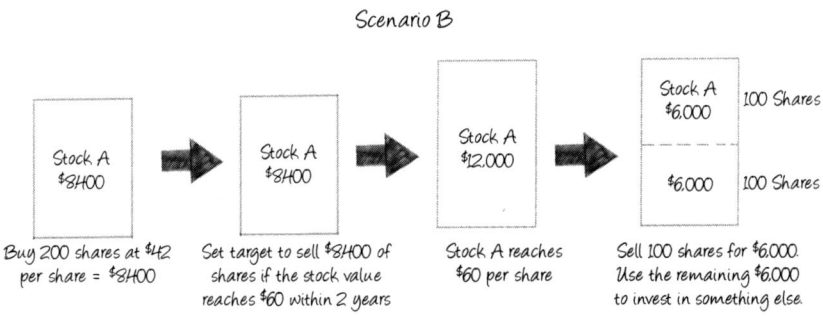

Scenario A)

- Buy 200 shares of Stock A at $42 per share, which is $8,400
- Set target to sell $8,400 of Stock A when the stock reaches $60 per share anytime within two years. (If it does not hit $60 within 2 years, she might set a new price, or she might change that sell price earlier)
- If the stock reaches that price and she sells, that leaves 60 shares at $60 per share, for a total of $3,600 "house money" still invested in Stock A. That also leaves her the original $8,400 available now to invest in another stock.

Remember – when you have cash, you have options.

OK, my sketches aren't the works of da Vinci, but I think you can follow the process, right? Keep in mind this is just a hypothetical example and Stock A is not a real company. You won't find Stock A stores at the mall selling Stock A brand crackers or Stock A label pants.

This example is based on the principles of having a plan before you buy, of selling when it's time to sell and of always playing with house money. You notice that Mom took out the exact amount she put in? What's left is house money, so she is now playing Stock A with house money.

Scenario B)

While this rule is valuable as a principle, there is no reason you can't fiddle with that a bit. For instance, you might instead decide to just sell 100 shares of Stock A and hang on to another 100. In that case, you would retain $6,000 invested in Stock A, and have $6,000 in cash ready to invest in something else.

Are you ready for a small complication? OK, here goes. Let's suppose that Stock A pays a 3% dividend. That would be $360 on $12,000 worth of shares (200 shares at $60 each). Let's further suppose that the dividend is paid semi-annually, which would amount to $180 every six months, and that the payment is effective one week after the stock reaches $60. Should Mom sell her shares right away?

If she waits a week, she'll make $180 in dividends, but she would be "cheating" on her plan to sell when they reach $60 per share. $180 is a lot to give up, and it is a sure thing.

On the other hand, the stock might go down after the dividend payout, or up further – whichever way it goes, it is not a sure thing.

There is no rule to this, but Mom generally waits for the dividend. The dividend is a sure thing, whereas the stock will fluctuate. If the stock remains above $60 after the dividend payout, she will sell. If it dips a bit, she will keep watching it, ready to sell when it hits $60 per share again.

So one of the things she is watching for on her laptop is which of her holdings is approaching that sell price, and also, how close those stocks are to their next dividend payout.

For a stock that pays 1%, Mom might not care as much about the dividend. For a stock that pays 5%, she might care much more about the dividend. In fact, if a company is strong and healthy with a 5% dividend, Mom will probably set a much higher sell price, and might not even plan to sell at all.

Can I throw in another complexity? Good, I knew you'd love a challenge. What happens if a stock suddenly takes off? What happens if Stock A goes from $42 to $60 within a week. That is a crazy rise. Who knows how high it will shoot up before it goes down? Suddenly this is not investing – it's gambling.

What does Mom do?

> *The first thing I do is stick to my plan. If my plan is to sell 140 shares when it hits $60 anytime within two years, that doesn't change.*

The fact that Mom sells within a month instead of within 19 or 20 months means that she makes a nice bonus. Do you know why selling Stock A for $60 a month after buying it is worth more than selling it 18 months later for that price?

First, after 18 months, inflation has already begun to eat into the value of that $60. But second, and more importantly, she now has her $8,400 18 months earlier to reinvest in another stock. That means 18 months more time for it to make money for her.

> *But I also formulate a new plan for what remains invested in Stock A. I have to decide what price I will sell them.*

Right, Mom. The stock has been climbing like crazy. You've sold what you planned to. What to do about the rest?

Mom might decide to sell the remaining shares in Stock A when they reach $70. They might not reach that price. They might stop at $61 and then go down. In that case, she holds onto them for a while longer. It might be a long while, but she never planned to sell them that fast anyway.

But Stock A might continue to climb. It might reach $75. Or $85. It might even break $100. Mom will sell at $70 because that is her plan. If she was to wait to see how high it would go, she could get caught in a free-fall, where people can't sell for their asking price, and take a loss. For instance, if she was to wait and the stock starts falling at $85, she could try selling at $80, but if she is not quick enough, it could be down at $65 by the time her sale goes through.

Mom is not a gambler. She's an investor. So she sells at the price she plans, and once she has sold the stock, it really doesn't matter what happens next. Once she has sold it, she has fulfilled her plan. She does not worry if it keeps rising. She does not wonder, "How much more money could I have made if I had just waited to sell a little longer?"

Nor does she worry about what happens in between. She sold some at $60. Her plan was to sell the rest at $70 if the stock reached that high. She did not worry about what happens when it hits $66. Or $67. Or $68. No nail biting required. She is watching, of course, because she wants to be ready, but she knows that she will sell if and when it hits $70, so she doesn't have to worry about it from one day to the next.

I said that "what happens next" doesn't matter. But that's not really true, for two reasons. It does matter what happens next because she now has $8,400 to invest. She needs to find a stock to invest in. Well, that's not completely true, either. She has a couple dozen stocks in mind, and she has spent some time each day watching them to see which of them might be approaching her buy price. If one of them has been around her buy price, she might decide to reinvest most of her $8,400 in that stock right away. Or she might hold onto the money until one of her wish-list stocks dips to the buy price.

Yes, I said "most of". Why? Because she tries to leave a bit or more in reserves, so that she is prepared if a great buying opportunity comes along.

The other reason that "what happens next" matters is that Stock A was a great stock. That's why she bought it in the first place. After all the craziness, and after she has sold her shares, she might place that company back on her watch list. She might want to buy the shares back at a lower price!

I know! This is so exciting! I get goose bumps.

All that up and down with Stock A was something temporary. She took her profit from it, but if the stock goes back to near her original buy price, she might just reinvest that $8,400 back in Stock A at the now-lower price. Or if she ended up selling all the shares, she might reinvest it all back in Stock A. It sounds crazy, right? She put the money in. She sold the shares to take the money out. Now she would put it back in. Where's the gain in that?

Let's sketch it out on another piece of napkin.

- Buy 200 shares at $42 per share for $8,400.
- Sell 100 shares at $60 per share for $6,000.
- Sell remaining 100 shares at $70 per share for $7,000.
- She now has $13,000 to re-invest. If she can buy shares once again at $42 per share, she will own 309 shares – 109 free shares.

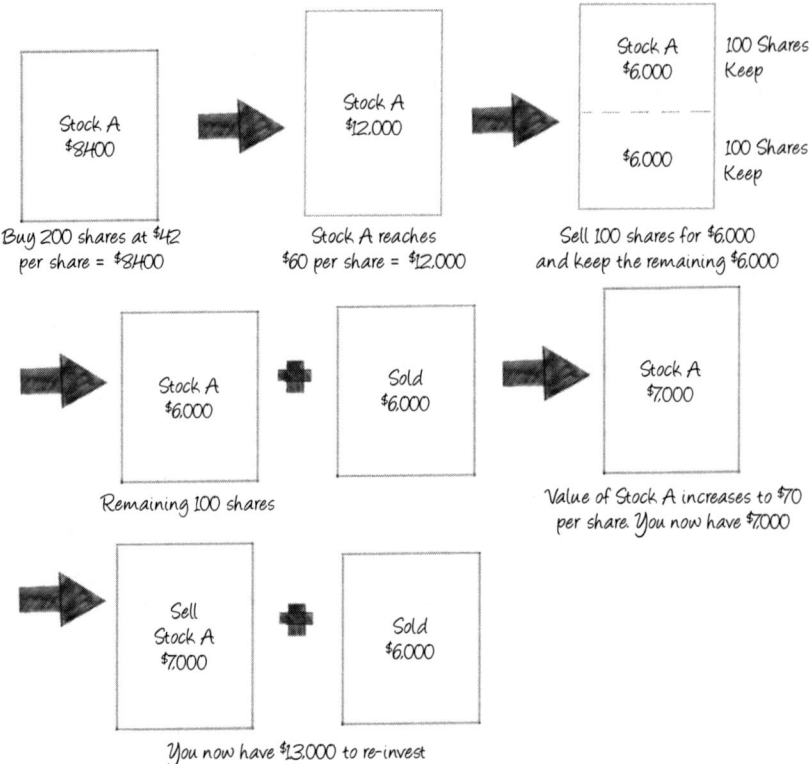

So the profit is that she owns more of the company. As those shares slowly climb back up to her $60 sell price, she'll make a lot more from selling 309 shares then she would have from selling 200 shares at that price – $6540 more, to be precise. She will make $18,540 instead of $12,000 if she sells them all at $60.

But to do all this, Mom has to keep track of the current prices of all her stocks and of all the stocks she is watching. So she is tracking how close each one gets to the buy or sell price. And she is also keeping track of how close each stock is to paying dividends.

Keep in mind that if a stock on Mom's wish-list is hovering very near to the buy price just before dividend payout, she might buy it anyway, because the dividend will make up for the small price gap.

Another thing Mom likes to watch for is news about companies on her wish list. That's because she buys when company stock dips.

> *I like to buy stock on my wish list when it drops by 10-20%. Even the best companies' stocks fall 10-20% from time to time.*

Sure, Mom. Dips happen for all kinds of crazy reasons. It could be a simple market correction. It could even be that the media had been expecting slightly higher profits in a quarter and the price dips on not meeting those expectations. It could be that the latest product release just did not catch fire. It could be that the CEO has resigned and there is nervousness at the temporary vacancy. Or some large hedge funds might have moved some money around and sold stock in the company to free up some cash.

These are all temporary jitters, and they present a great buying opportunity for investors like Mom. We know that the stock will head back on its upward trajectory before too long. This is when Mom knows it's a good time to get in, when there is a sudden adjustment – a dip.

> *When this happens, I make sure to see check company news to see if the reasons for the dip are not life-threatening to the company. The reasons can be anything, as you said, Victor. As long as I feel the company will not go bankrupt and will continue to make money well into the future, I buy it, and there is no better time.*

This is exactly what Trevor Ewen did. He is a partner at Neosavvy, a tech consultancy based out of New York. He recalls one episode where his holdings appeared to take a hit: "Monday was a very good example of this. I own a lot of ETFs comprising many REITs so I felt much of the shock. My plan really was not to panic and to look at common sense and fundamentals. It went down 14% in half an hour, but my investment was all US-based real estate. Just because the concern was a slight devaluing of the Chinese currency overseas doesn't mean US real estate is in trouble. So what did I do? I bought. My plan has always been to recognize a good asset when people act irrationally."

> *Trevor is a smart man. He looked at fundamentals. He looked at the facts. He ignored the foolish opinions driving the market that day, and he stuck to the facts.*

When you are buying a long-term investment, who cares about the temporary jitters. They won't shake you. But they do give you a chance to buy the stock for a discount, which means you can buy more stock than you might have been able to a week earlier, and so you make more money when you sell. Remember that example with Stock A? If you can buy more stock with your money, you make more profit, as we saw when we tortured ourselves with a bit of fun math on Stock A.

So company news is very important because Mom needs to know what is happening, even if she ignores most of the news. The key is that she does triage. In one pile she places all the news that is nothing but gossip and passing happenings. In the other pile … well, there isn't another pile. If she does see news that is life-threatening to a company, she would act on it. She would either sell if she owns the stock, or remove the company from her watch list if she doesn't.

Remember that very little news really is life-threatening to a company. Even major catastrophes like the BP oil spill or the Exxon Valdez oil spill, or like Detroit needing to be bailed out in the 2008 recession, did not spell death or even long-term injury for the companies involved. Business continues as strong as ever because people still need oil and they still need cars. They might hate BP and call them names for what happened in the Gulf of Mexico, but they still buy the oil they need.

AN HOUR IN THE LIFE OF MOM | 183

And so it is with all the types of companies Mom buys — indispensable supplies that people rely on in good times and bad.

When those kinds of companies dip 10-20%, Mom buys. But what if she owns the stock, and let's say it dips by 25% or even by 50%

> *Wow, Victor, are you trying to scare our guest? I buy only blue chip stocks. Didn't you already tell our guest never to buy speculative stocks that bounce around like that? A case of a blue chip stock dropping by 50% would be pretty rare.*

You are right, Mom. But let's say a stock drops by 50%, precisely because that is a good way to scare our guest. You see, any stock can drop at any moment for any reason by any amount. And there are plenty of stocks that do drop by 50% in a week. That's why it is so important to buy only the types of solid stocks we have been talking about these past nine sessions.

A lot of people would panic at a 50% drop. The sky is falling! The sky is falling! And they sell. But I know Mom won't sell because she has faith in the stocks she buys. She knows they are solid. She knows they are keepers. Like that word? "Keepers." She keeps those stocks, even if they fall.

Why? Because she hasn't actually lost any money. That's the miracle about stocks. You don't lose money until you sell them. So just hang onto them until they go back up in value. But what if they dip by 50% That's a lot. Can we look for a moment at what Mom would do?

> *Sure. I do the same research I would before buying a stock that has just dipped. I would find out why it has dipped and ask myself if the reasons are life-threatening. If they aren't, I might just buy some more stock in the company and increase my holdings.*

Aha! That is clever thinking. If it's a buying opportunity when stocks you don't own dip, it's just as much of a buying opportunity when stocks you own dip. And using the example of a 50% dip, which gives us the opportunity to lower the price we bought our investments for.

Consider this. We bought 100 shares of Stock B at $10 per share (or $1000 total), and now the price dips by 50%, so we buy another 100 shares at $5 each (or $500 total). That brings the average cost per share down from $10 to $7.50.

Let's suppose the stock price rises back up to $10 per share a month later. Mom would then sell off her initial 100 shares for $10 each, or $1000 in total. There is no profit there, but it does free up $1000 to invest in other stock opportunities.

She would be left with 100 shares, as she had before the stock fell. And they would still be worth $1000 as they were before the stock fell. But her cost to buy that $1000 of shares is only $500. What a deal!

> *What is really, really important is to make sure that the reasons the stock fell are not life-threatening. If they are temporary, there will be an upswing to profit from. But if they are life-threatening, there will be no upswing.*

And that's much of what Mom does during her daily hour on the laptop, check for life-threatening news.

> *The other important thing is that I buy more stock only if it falls below my planned buying price.*

Right. So if you have bought shares in Company B at $10, and the stock rises to $20 per share, and then it dips to $15, Mom would not buy it. Why? Because it hasn't dipped enough. It hasn't dipped below her $10 buying level. Of course, if the rise from $10 to $20 happened over the course of four years, she might have changed her buy price for the stock. That price really needs to be revised every year or two, anyway.

As Mom pointed out, most blue chip stocks don't just plunge 50%. It can happen – anything can happen! – but it's pretty rare. More often a stock might simply languish, like a turtle on the beach, not doing too much of anything. It might very slowly drop over the course of a couple years, or it might just move sideways, never really changing much from one year to the next (except that inflation makes that same price worth less, of course).

In such cases, the dividends usually cover things. A dividend of 3-4% makes a solid company worth holding over the long term. That dividend represents the company's profits, distributed to its owners. As long as there are profits, there will be dividends.

> *What I noticed about stocks before steep rises is they usually have a long period of sideways movement before exploding upward. With the dividend, you get paid to wait in the meantime. You have to have patience in this game. You will lose if you don't.*

Mom, you're more chatty than usual today.

> *Well, you've joined me while I'm sitting at my laptop, so I'm here at the table instead of moving about the kitchen, as I usually am.*

So you are. I guess that's what can happen to stock, as well. Sometimes they can move about quite a bit, but other times they just don't move a lot at all.

Mom is right. It can be a waiting game. Sometimes a stock just sits there, and for no explicable reason, one day just starts moving. That is another reason why picking dividend stocks is so important, so as to make money while the stock is sitting.

> *There are some stocks that I call core stocks. And it's OK if they sit. I buy them with no intention to sell them, although I might from time to time sell if there is a good selling opportunity.*

Ah yes, those would be stocks like banks and life insurance companies, transportation and utilities, the long-term pillars of our economy.

> *Right. I used the profits from my Coach and Under Armour shares only to build up my core stocks, because banks and utilities don't go out of style.*

So Mom doesn't need to spend as much time tracking those core stocks in her daily hour as she does tracking consumer product stocks, partly also because there are more consumer product companies to watch.

What is interesting is that when Mom sees something on that laptop of hers that is ripe for buying, she always seems to be able to buy it. She always seems to have cash on hand. Doesn't that make you wonder? Who's feeding her money whenever she needs it? Doesn't that make you curious?

OK, you've twisted my arm. I'll tell you how Mom can afford to always buy the stock she wants when she wants. The secret is in one word.

> *Reserves.*[12]

---

[12] Reserves are your funds that are on standby and is only used in a buying opportunity. Reserves can be from anywhere: they can be money that is not used immediately from a stock sale, a part of your paycheque you had the discipline to deposit into your investment account, or even money you found underneath your living room couch. Simply put, reserves are funds in your account that make it possible for you to keep pouncing onto stock opportunity after stock opportunity. Therefore, I encourage everyone to make a habit of maintaining a healthy reserve as it's an integral part of your portfolio – so look under your couch often!

Mom always keeps reserves on hand. Let's suppose she has $20,000 to invest. Stock C becomes available at the price she wants, do you think she buys $20,000 of Stock C shares? As you probably guessed by now, she does not. She might invest $15,000, and hold back the remaining $5,000 in reserves, just in case the perfect opportunity arises. Remember that she never borrows to buy stock; that's a pretty important rule she follows, to never invest money she cannot afford to lose.

Those reserves will be bolstered the next time she sells stock, but in the meantime, she at least has that $5,000 available, in case a stock she is watching makes an opportune dip.

And you will notice that we have taken emotion out from the equation. You see that, right? We are watching for actual facts to happen. We buy on facts. We sell on facts. We have the downside covered, so we have no need to panic.

> *After going through the rigors of selecting the stock, the hard part is done. The fun part for me is watching it go up and making money.*

Did you notice something else clever about Mom's strategy? Clever it is, and so counterintuitive, too. When the price of her stock rises, she sells. Not just on any price rise, mind you. Remember that she has a plan even before buying a stock. She plans at exactly what price to sell how much of it.

And when the price of her stock falls, she buys more of it. And again, not just any price drop. She sticks to her plan and buys only when it dips below a certain price. This is all very methodological. No emotions, just facts. No fear. No greed. No panic. And no need for a manicure to cover up those nails she might otherwise be biting.

> *Oh, I don't worry about my nails. I do my morning stretches, and I go for my daily walks.*

And Mom sits down at her computer one hour a day. Just one hour. And here we are in Vancouver, with the markets in Toronto and New York City opening at 6 a.m. our time. That is a huge time difference to overcome.

> *Well, I certainly don't pull out my laptop at 6 a.m. In fact, I don't pull it out until 9:00 in the morning. That's my hour on my laptop. I don't worry about when there's an opening bell or a closing bell. I do this on my own time. After that, the only bells I'll be interested in are bell peppers.*

Right. Because those bells are for traders, not for investors.

Mom sets up automatic buy and sell orders online. So when a stock's price hits that buy-price or that sell-price, it's done for her while she sleeps. Or while she shops.

> *Or while my son takes me out to see a show.*

Oh, I think I'm getting a hint. I promised Mom a movie right after our meeting today. So the point is that when you have a game plan, when you know at what price you plan to buy and sell, you don't have to be in front of your computer screen watching what happens. When the price is right, the order will execute.

You might wonder why Mom needs to be here every day and watch as the stock value gets close to her sell price if an automated order will sell it for her anyway. What does she need to be prepared for? Well, there are a couple things that we have already talked about. If a dividend payout is coming up, she might choose to delay the sell order for another week. So she needs to pay attention to that.

Also, if she is about to cash in some stock, she will want to know what other stocks are approaching her buy prices. She might have some choices and she might have a preference as to which stock she wants to buy next, or whether she wants to keep the proceeds of the sale as cash reserves.

And, of course, she is watching closely to be sure that none of her stocks or her wish-list are making any life-threatening boo boos.

So a lot of what Mom does in her daily hour is to review her orders and make sure they are still valid and tweak them if it makes sense to. And she wants to make sure she is ready to make choices and logical decisions. Every now and then it is important to review and revise one's sell price or even one's buy price, in which case automated orders must also be replaced.

But that's not all Mom watches for in her hour daily. She is also watching for consumer trends and other trend-type news. She wants to know how the world is changing over time because that will have a huge effect on the types of companies that might go in and out of style. She doesn't invest in Moat Diggers Inc. anymore for that very reason. Not too many people need moats dug around their castles these days.

Well, it looks like Mom's hour is almost up, and so is ours. It went so fast, I forgot to offer you tea or anything to eat. So sorry about that, but I was very excited to give you a first-hand look into exactly what Mom does with her daily investing hour and how valuable it can be for making buy and sell decisions.

Okay, time for me to go buy those tickets now for tonight. See you next time!

WHAT YOU LEARNED ON THIS VISIT

What to watch for daily on the Internet

How a stock buy and sell plan looks

How to stick to your plan

How dividends can affect a selling choice

What to do if stock you own falls in price

The importance of cash reserves

The power of automation

CHAPTER 10
The Recipe

> *"Dealing with complexity is an inefficient and unnecessary waste of time, attention, and mental energy. There is never any justification for things being complex when they could be simple."*
>
> —Dr. Edward de Bono

Hello and welcome back!

How was the movie you ask? Oh, it was great. The popcorn always brings back my childhood.

It's unfortunate you won't be able to stay with us too long today. Mom understands we are all busy. She also understands if you're forgetful and need a recap or a reminder. You're always welcome to revisit our lessons and to have our tasty treats but here's Mom's investing recipe in a nutshell.

Keep in mind that this recipe is not carved in stone. As with any recipe, you can experiment with the ingredients. Any good chef knows that once you know the logic and principle behind cooking, you can create your own magic in the kitchen, but only after you have mastered the logic. Even Mom deviates from the recipe occasionally. That said, the principles should be followed at all times.

Play it how it is intended to be played

The game of stocks can be very complicated or very simple – it depends on how you view it. How I see it, the freshest ingredients and simplest cooking methods yield the best results. Do not be mistaken: simple does not mean easy. It takes years of learning and discipline to achieve what Mom has done. She knows of only one way to win in stocks:

Use House Money to build your stock empire by REINVESTING your gains in existing stocks and in new stocks. That's it. In fact, Mom's investing recipe is a lot like her grocery shopping! Don't believe me? Let's explore.

Groceries first.

Get Organized

Before stepping into a grocery store it's wise to create a shopping list. Here's the scenario: Imagine you're hosting your annual backyard roast for family and friends. You will most likely find yourself in a conundrum: will you serve ribeye or sirloin? Russet or yellow gold potato? Salad with romaine or iceberg lettuce? Being aware of what ingredients are available is as important as keeping them organized.

Get to know the supermarket departments

When you walk into the grocery store, you see an astonishing range of foods, from cereals to meats, fruits to dairy, sweets to vegetables. Certainly you're not going to buy and eat all 90 kinds of bread they sell, right? And that's just the bakery. There's also the produce department, the butcher, the deli, and so many more sections. Some grocery stores may have a specialized sushi department which others may lack. So you must familiarize yourself with the different sections of the store to know where to get the foods you need for that balanced feast.

Fill your shopping cart with quality foods

As you walk around the store you see all the different promotions on flyers, discounts here and there, and if you're lucky, employees handing out tasty samples of their latest treats. Many things can sidetrack you, remember that you are on a mission!

You focus and make your way to the meat section.

You are now staring at the two cuts (ribeye and sirloin) with one question in mind: Which one to choose? We must base our decision on a number of criteria. You inspect them by seeing if they have the right marbling, the right texture and firmness, and whether or not they smell funny. Funny is good on TV; funny is not good in the meat aisle.

Funny is even worse with stocks.

Buy at a discount

Having inspected both the ribeye and sirloin you find that both are equal in terms of quality, so which cut should you buy? Mom says to look at the prices. Generally, ribeye is a more expensive cut than sirloin, however there's a promotion happening. It's now 20% off! Fantastic, I think today you should go with the ribeye.

Just as Mom loves to discount shop in the supermarket, she loves to discount shop in the stock market. The best deals are the quality ones you snatch up at a discount.

Now stock investing.

Step 1: Get organized

You must create your own 'shopping list' or 'watchlist' so that you can organize your stocks and see how they're doing at all times. Track them by registering an online tracker. Go and sign up. Here are a few free trackers I like to use:

1. The Globe and Mail: *http://www.theglobeandmail.com/globe-investor/my-watchlist/*
2. Bloomberg: *http://www.bloomberg.com/markets/watchlist*
3. Google Finance: *https://www.google.ca/finance/portfolio*

Download the Bloomberg app on your phone, that's my favorite to use. Although there are premium trackers that charge monthly subscription fees, they aren't necessary for our purpose.

Keep in mind that when you register for an actual online trading account, it will most likely come with a tracker. However, I use one outside of my real account so that I can quickly have access to my stocks anywhere with my phone without the hassle and security issues of logging in and out of my real one.

Step 2: Get to know the stock market sectors

There is a mind-boggling array of stocks to choose from. They can be divided into different sectors, different capitalization, different dividends, and different histories. Where does one start? With thousands of companies you can throw your money at, Mom suggests that you start by looking at her list.

To maintain a balanced diet of sectors in your shopping list, here is Mom's own list from which to choose from (sector – and some examples)[13]:

---

[13] Chapter 6, page 124 for descriptions of these sectors

1 Financials – banks and insurance companies.
2 Infrastructure – railroads, roads, port facilities, and pipelines.
3 Energy/Utilities – gas producers and power plants.
4 Food – food and beverage manufactures.
5 Real Estate – office towers, malls and warehouses.
6 Medical/Healthcare – drug, hospital supply, and medical diagnostic equipment manufacturers.
7 Basic Materials – aluminum, steel, and chemical manufacturers.
8 Non-cyclical goods and services – breweries, wineries, tobacco, household products, and entertainment.
9 Cyclical goods and services – apparel, advertising, hotels, restaurants, computers and electronics.
10 Telecommunications – telephone companies, network providers, and satellites we use to exchange information.
11 Transportation – aerospace, airlines, freight and courier, and car manufacturers.
12 Technology – semiconductors, software, information technology service and consulting, and hardware.

These are the 12 sectors Mom has identified for you as being those our modern lives cannot be without. Once you are familiar with these sectors and the companies within them, you will see how to diversify your portfolio. So, go ahead first and pick 4-5 sectors from this list.

Step 3: Fill your shopping list with quality companies

Similar to choosing her meats, Mom pokes and prods her stocks too before she buys them. She wants to buy only great companies – companies that will make money and with almost no risk of losing long term money. She doesn't want any stocks that smell funny.

To find the companies we want, let's use a stock screener. Here are a few screeners I like:

1. The Globe and Mail: *http://www.theglobeandmail.com/globe-investor/portfolio-and-tools/screener/*
2. Google Finance: *https://www.google.ca/finance/stockscreener*
3. Financial Visualizations: *http://finviz.com/screener.ashx*[14]

Each screener is a little different and offers a variety of search parameters. Whichever one you use, get to know them by playing around with them and select the one you feel comfortable with.

Here are some specifics to look for. This is not meant as a substitute for really studying stocks and understanding the details, but it will help you quickly separate the good companies from the bad. It's what Mom and I call the basic "10/10/10/10" criteria:

a Does the stock have over $10 billion market capitalization?[15]

b Does the stock have over $10/share price?

c Does the stock have over 10-year history?

d Has the stock paid reliable dividends for over 10 years?

Look at the search results and do your best to find these answers for each stock. Put the stock in your watch list if you answer 'yes' to questions 'a' through 'd'.[16] Compile about 15-20 stocks in your watch list. Identify which sectors your companies fall under and make sure you have a good mix. Get to know these stocks like an old friend.

---

[14] I like finviz.com particularly because their comprehensive screener can easily filter by market capitalization, dividend, and even sector and industry so you can effectively manage diversifying your searches.

[15] Over $1 billion in market capitalization should you choose to buy ETFs, income funds, and income trusts.

[16] Entering an unusual value for market capitalization such as $13 or $17 billion and dividend yield such as 1.3% or 4.2% may provide a unique list of attractive companies

Once you have established your diversified list comprising of 15-20 stocks, it is now crucial to write down per stock 1 logical reason why they are on your list.

The more specific your reasons the better. Here's an example:

A not-so good reason: *I like BMO because their branches offer coffee and I love coffee.*

A better reason: *I like BMO because it's one of Canada's most reliable lenders and I have a savings account with them.*

A great reason: *I like BMO because they have consistently paid out dividends to their shareholders for the past 186 years and this company aligns with my goal to diversify into the financial sector.*

This is because no matter how good a stock looks, it's not worth having if you can't even give yourself one more reason to own it. Your answers should be based on why you believe your stocks are going to be profitable over the next decade. It may not be easy to find reasons to jot down at first. Only by researching does that force you to dive in to learn about the company. Discard the stocks you don't have reasons for and look for other ones that do.

Once you have the reasons to all your 15-20 stocks, they will eventually become the "quality" companies you will buy.

Step 4: Buy at a discount

With a shopping list on hand, Mom says, "A good entry point of a stock is when it experiences a quick selloff of 10-20%. Just like groceries, I love buying quality stocks at a discount. Remember, as you see stocks selloff, opportunities start to emerge. You are a contrarian now, not a member of the herd."

It is not necessary to track your stock's movement every day. We're here to invest, not trade. Focusing on the day-to-day movements of a stock is unnecessary, so kick up your feet and only look at them once a week. It's better for your sanity that way.

Step 5: Playing the game.

For each stock, commit to a decision by stating, "If the stock hits '*U price*' within '*V months/years*', I will sell '*W amount*'" and "If the stock hits '*X price*' within '*Y months/years*', I will buy '*Z amount*'". We call those prices *action targets*: a "sell" price is a price above your average stock purchase price, whereas a "buy" price is a price below your average stock purchase price. An action target must include 3 things: a *price*, a *quantity*, and *a period of time*. It therefore becomes your commitment to take action within that period of time you set.

What price and quantity of shares and length of time you set as your action targets is not as important as the act of following through with it – do not set impossible action targets or else you will never buy or sell! Likewise, if you set targets too close, you may buy and sell too often!

Also, before you buy any stock to expand your portfolio, make sure you are:

a Diversifying (buying into other sectors)
b Holding 30% of total portfolio in reserve (cash) after initial purchase
c Buying stock on your shopping list at a 10-20% bargain

If your time action target is set at 1 year and after that year no action target is reached, you shall re-evaluate to adjust the prices and set new ones for that stock.

Here is an example of setting action targets:

The price of ABC Co. stock on your shopping list drops from $24 → 20 (17% change), and you decide to buy in at this point.

You use $1000 to buy 50 shares (for this example we will disregard trading fees). You then set action targets: *(see diagram below)*

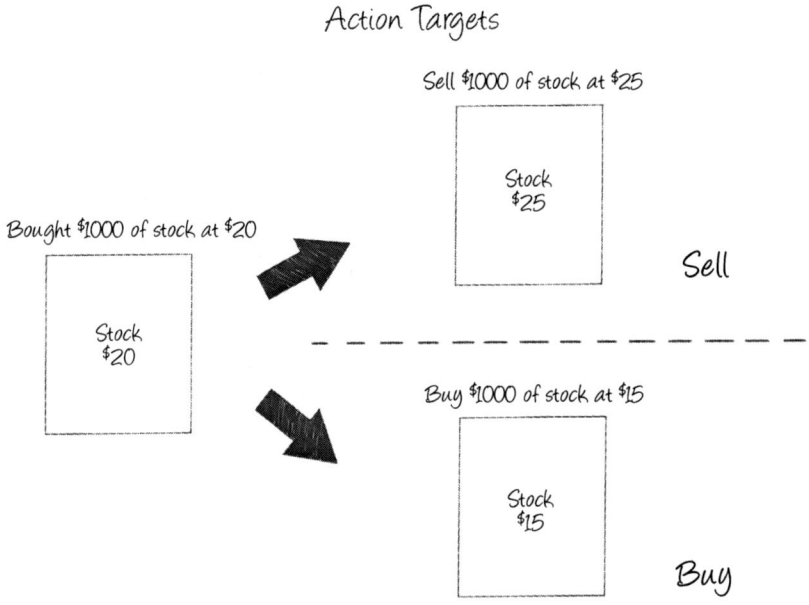

If the share price of ABC Co. reaches **$25** within your set time period, your 'sell' action target is reached. Do the following: *(see diagram on next page)*

a Execute your selling
You **sell** $1000 (40 shares) of stock and let the remaining 10 shares sit and grow. You now own $250 or 10 shares of house money.

b Your $1000 original investment shall return to the reserve to be ready for the next purchase opportunity at a discount.

c Now set your new action targets based on your new stock price. For example, since our new stock price is $25, we may set our sell action target to $27 for the remaining 10 shares or to not sell at all. Conversely, our buy action target may be to buy $700 of stock (leaving 30% in reserve) at $23 or to keep our $1000 original investment for other purchases.

New Action Targets

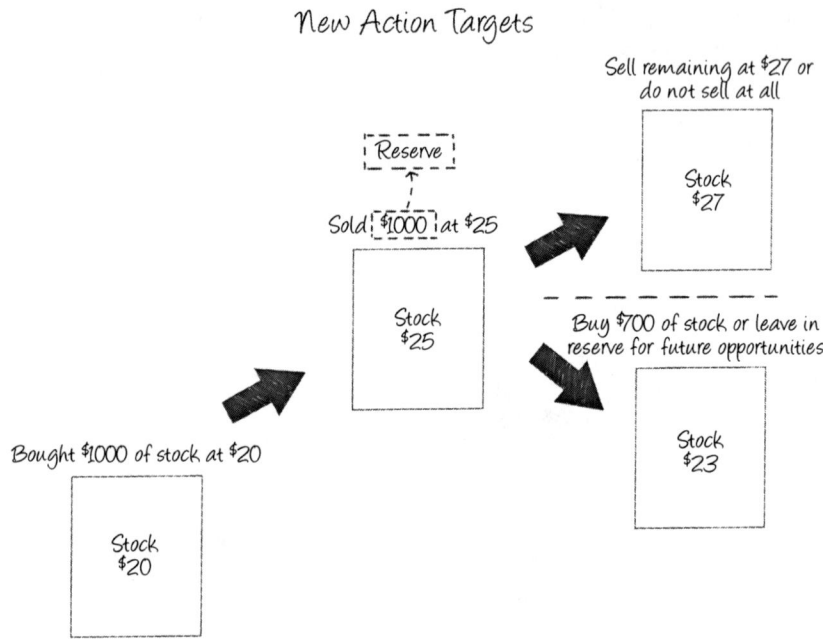

If, however, the share price goes down to **$15** within your set time period, your 'buy' action target is reached. Do the following: *(see diagram on next page)*

a Execute your buying
You **buy** $1000 (66 shares) of stock. The cost of owning more of this stock is less now.

b Because now that you have bought in more than once, your average purchase price is now lower than $20. On your online brokerage account, it will calculate your average purchase price for you. In this example, average price went from $20 to $17.24[17] now. The average purchase price is important because it is your breakeven point. If the current stock price is higher than your average purchase, you can make money by selling. If it is below, you will lose money by selling.

---

[17] To calculate average purchase price, take the total dollar amount divided by total number of shares. In this example, $1000/@20 = 50 shares & $1000/@15 = 66 shares, so 50 + 66 = 116 total shares purchased. $1000 + $1000 = $2000 total dollar amount, so $2000/116 = $17.24 average purchase price.

c Now set your new action targets based on your new average purchase price. For example, our average price is $17.24, we may set our sell action target to sell $1500 at $19 per share to make a profit of $1.76 per share. Conversely, our buy action target may be to buy $200 of stock at $13 per share thus lowering our average purchase price again. Don't forget, these action targets are set by you to make sure that you follow through with your commitment to take action.

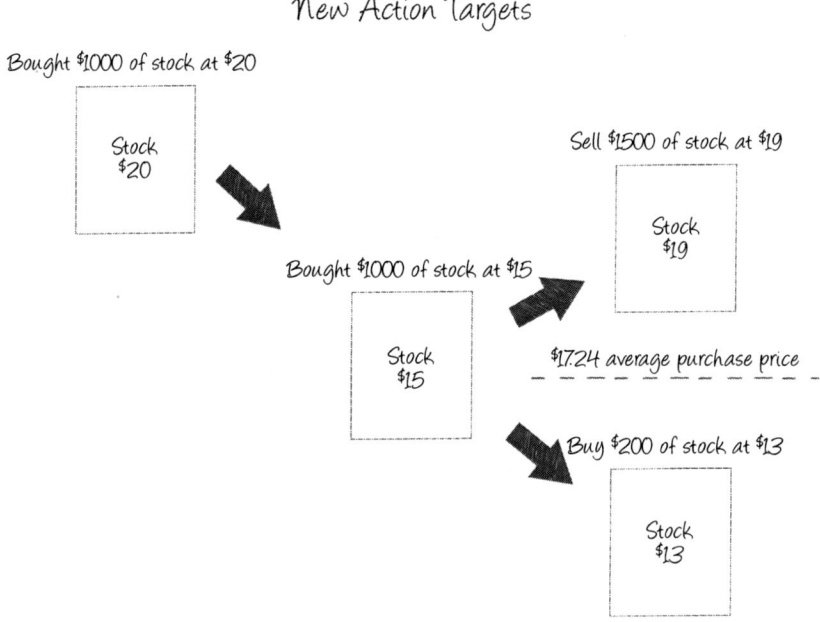

In general, the wider the range you have your action targets ($25 and $15 targets are $10 apart), the more profitable you will be and less day to day tracking you will need. In contrast, action targets of say, $22 and $18, will require more monitoring. Remember to also set new time periods for every new action targets set.

Steps 1 – 3 are to protect your downside. Steps 4 – 5 is to take advantage of the upside!

Stay disciplined and methodical. Leave emotions out.

Step 6: Mom's Simplified Expansion Recipe:

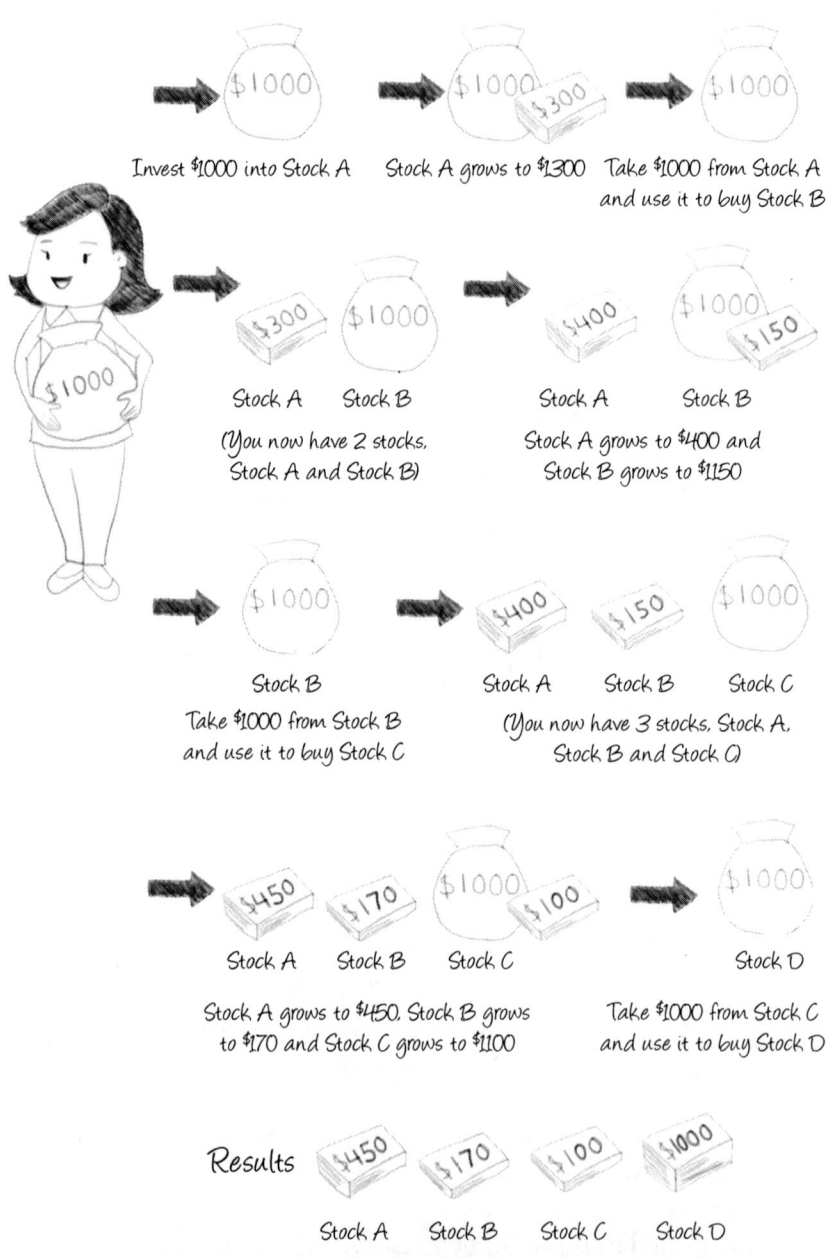

To put it all together, I want to show you AGAIN the example of how successful planning and execution with action targets can get you 4 companies all from the same $1000 investment. In concept, this is what she used to turn just 3 bank stocks in 2006 into owning 46 blue chip stocks today.

This is using house money to grow your fortune. Any amount that you gain and leave in a stock is house money.

Removing your initial investment to play solely on house money is in theory, the most ideal situation. However, it can often be challenging to do it all at once. Rather than selling your initial investment all in one shot as in the example, you can sell off smaller chunks on the way up while setting various action targets. That's okay. You want to take as much of the original investment capital out of the stock as possible when you sell, leaving your house money inside. The whole purpose of Mom's recipe is to reuse your original investment again and again.

So, the way to win in the stock market game is to: Use house money to build your stock empire by REINVESTING your original money into new stocks and into existing stocks. Buy, sell, take out original investment, set action target, repeat. Mom's success is common sense: she makes her plans based on facts, then she sticks to it.

Just like everything worth doing in life, this takes practice. And now that you know her recipe, you can do it too!

Exit strategy

Remember those reasons you wrote down for each stock from Step 3? At least once a month, Mom sits at the kitchen table on her laptop to review those reasons she wrote down for each stock she bought. You should too.

Glance over the stocks news to make sure they remain aligned with the reasons you wrote down.

If the news and reports are bad, then evaluate whether the direction of the company is life-threatening to the company's stock. Ask yourself this question: "Is it a recoverable change or an unrecoverable change?" Even most tragedies that companies experience are recoverable. They usually drive down the value of the stock, which means that you can buy it at a discount.

Corporate tragedy = buying opportunity.

On rare occasions when a company's news or direction is unrecoverable, it is not a buying opportunity. It's time to get out, regardless of action targets.

An example of this is the Polaroid Corporation which had failed to transition its imaging and photography business into the digital age. Such an example is not only as rare as getting hit by lightning, but also shows that there was ample time for investors to take notice and get out.

What will happen tomorrow?

Remember, there is big money – HUGE money – invested in sidetracking you. Do not listen to people's predictions anywhere. Resist the tasty morsels. Always remember to look at the facts and formulate your own decisions without being influenced by others. Baseless predictions lead to emotions and emotions often lead you down the wrong path. More importantly, they will only sidetrack you from your objective of making money. The market isn't predictable because people react to news unpredictably. And those people lose a lot of money by reacting. Market movements are driven by the complex actions and emotions of people. Since we cannot control human emotions, we must leave out trying to predict the movements of stocks. The most sensible thing we can do is read about the facts of the companies we invest in. Because who really knows what will happen tomorrow?

Conclusion: You Get Rich

> *Money is better than poverty, if only for financial reasons.*
>
> —Woody Allen

Welcome back for your final visit. I am going to miss you. But this is an exciting moment because this is the conclusion. This is the result of all our discussions, of all your studying, of all the challenges … and of several pots of tea.

Ooh, speaking of which, let me just head over to the counter and grab the kettle.

Mom also left a tray of sought after oatmeal cookies for us to munch on while we quickly review how you are about to get rich.

Has a healthy ring to it, doesn't it?

Your objective is to own as many top-quality "Mom" stocks (what she calls her "core" stocks) as possible in your lifetime, without ever borrowing money, playing with house money as soon as each stock earns enough in value to buy into another company.

That's all this is about. Mom's recipe is exactly that – a recipe. It is simple. It is common sense. It is a way to build wealth gradually over time, in a fairly predictable and risk-free way.

Here again is the process to follow:

1. Buy Stock A.
2. Stock A price rises > sell some Stock A
3. Use Stock A proceeds to buy Stock B
4. Stock B rises > sell some Stock B
5. Use proceeds to buy stock C
6. Stock C rises > sell some Stock C

By now, you already know to spend some time each day to watch your stocks to see which of them might be approaching your buy price. When you sell Stock A, you will already have a stock in mind, Stock B. And when you sell Stock B, you will already have a Stock C in mind, and so forth.

You also know better than to let emotions interfere in stock purchasing and selling decisions. You know that you need to be strong like Mom, sticking to your plan, no matter if the traders and gamblers are panicking in the streets. You have learned that you should be an investor, not a trader – that you should buy quality stock and just hold onto it.

Are you ready to be strong, like Mom? To hold onto your stock when people around you aren't even holding onto their heads?

In fact, you should know better than to give serious thought to selling at all. If you've made good buying decisions, let the stock do its roller coaster game. Let it tease and torment somebody else. And if other people foolishly sell in a misinformed panic, just say "Thank you" and help them sell by being their buyer.

While the stocks are doing what stocks do, you have a life to live. You might have a full-time job. You might have kids. You might have things you want to do with family or on your own, for charity or for fun. Make a little time to keep track of your stock, but if you go into each stock purchase with a plan and you set up automated sell orders based on that plan, you don't really need to even spend an hour a day keeping track of all your stocks.

Remember that the first goal is to become wealthy; the second goal is to have fun. If you follow Mom's recipe, you remove all the stress, and you have fun. Watching money accumulate is always fun. It's like a game that you always win.

And what is exciting for folks like you and me, is that we can win. We don't need to have a fancy education to score on the stock market. We don't even need special math skills. We simply need a common-sense approach that lets us accumulate wealth.

Mom doesn't have any special skills or education. She is just a typical housewife in a typical house, and she watches her stocks from this typical kitchen table. This is something anybody can do. This is something that can make anybody wealthy. And I am so excited that it will be making you wealthy.

And you can do it yourself. You don't need a broker to hold your hand. Just do it! You just have to remember the three magic words:

- Facts.
- Planning.
- Discipline.

You must base all your decisions on the facts, not on fear or greed or wishful thinking. You must plan carefully so that you know how much you are willing to pay for a stock and at what point you will sell it. And you must stick to the plan and not get swayed along the way by fear or greed or wishful thinking.

With your discipline, you can be an investor, not a trader. An investor is in it for the long term. You put your money in, and you watch it grow. A trader puts the money in, and is itching to sell as soon as possible. A trader tries to time the market. A trader is a bit of a gambler.

A trader is not an investor. But you already know that, and you are ready to ride the market, rather than try to beat the market. Good for you!

And you now know that a soaring stock is sell signal, not a buy signal. And that a falling stock is a buy signal not a sell signal. Most people have it all backwards, but you are smarter than most people. Like Warren Buffett, you can get stocks at a discount and sell them for a profit if you understand this one key concept, and include it in your plan.

So we come to the conclusion when it is time to say goodbye.

Don't forget to write. I really want to hear your success story. Because the conclusion of this story is "You get rich!"

MOM'S RECIPES

It just won't be Wall Street Kitchen without Mom's other recipes. If you've been wondering about them why not try making them at home for yourself?

PAN-FRIED WONTONS
(from Chapter 1)

Sister and I gather around the kitchen table to help mom wrap the wontons. Our wontons are normally prepared in batches and placed in the freezer so they can be enjoyed anytime.

Ingredients

(Makes about 40 wontons.)
½ lb (225 g) peeled, deveined shrimp, chopped
½ lb (225 g) lean ground pork
1 egg
2 tsp soy sauce
2 green onion, chopped
½ tsp sesame oil
A scant ¼ tsp ground white pepper
Pinch salt
About 40 square wonton wrappers
Dipping sauce ingredients:
Tube of wasabi
Mayonnaise

Method

In a bowl, combine egg, shrimp, pork, soy sauce, green onion, sesame oil, pepper and salt. Use a spoon-sized portion onto a wonton square wrapper and fold ends together. Use a dash of water to stick wonton ends together. Place wontons onto saran wrapped plate (to prevent sticking).

Place plates of wontons in a freezer until frozen. Place into plastic bags for later consumption.

When you want to eat them, remove them from the freezer and place frozen wontons in a pot of boiling water to cook. Gently separate wontons in water. When wontons float on water, they are cooked. In an oiled pan, bring to high heat and place cooked wontons into a pan. Fry wontons until crispy on one side. Remove from heat and serve on a plate. Sprinkle with chopped green onions. Mix 1 part wasabi to 3 parts mayonnaise for dipping.

GROUND BEEF SPAGHETTI
(from Chapter 2)

My childhood favorite after school meal!

Ingredients

1 lb lean ground beef
½ lb sliced fresh mushrooms
1 small onion, chopped
2 cans diced tomatoes, undrained
1 can tomato paste
1 can tomato sauce
2 tbsp dried parsley flakes
1 tsp dried basil
1 tsp dried oregano
1 tsp salt
¼ tsp pepper
Healthy pinch of fenugreek leaves
Hot cooked spaghetti

Method

In a large, deep, non-stick skillet, cook the beef, mushrooms and onion over medium heat until meat is no longer pink; drain.

Stir in the tomatoes, tomato paste, tomato sauce, parsley, basil, oregano, fenugreek leaves, salt and pepper. Cover and cook on low heat for 1-2 hours or until desired consistency. Serve over spaghetti. Sprinkle with cheese if desired.

VINDALOO CHICKEN
(from Chapter 3)

This recipe was often prepared on special occasions either when guests are over or during holidays.

Ingredients

Vindaloo Paste

1 tsp ground cumin
1 tsp ground turmeric
1 or 2 tsp garam masala
¼ tsp ground cinnamon
2 tsp mustard powder
1 tsp ground coriander
1 tsp cayenne pepper
2 cm cube of peeled ginger
3 tbsp white wine vinegar
1 tsp sugar

Vindaloo Base

150ml vegetable oil
4-8 garlic cloves, blended
3 red onions, preferably blended

Other Ingredients

5 red chillies, chopped finely
4 skinless chicken breasts cut into bite size pieces
500g good quality chopped tomatoes or chopped tinned tomatoes
1-2 tbsp of tomato purée to taste
1-4 tsp hot chilli powder to taste
Salt and pepper to taste

Method

Grate or slice the ginger finely and add the cumin, cinnamon, mustard, coriander turmeric, garam masala and cayenne pepper into a bowl and add the vinegar and sugar and mix thoroughly.

Heat the oil in a wok or large frying pan. Add the garlic and the onion and cook over a medium heat until they have softened for approx 5-7 mins, but take care not to let them burn or brown too much.

Once the onion and garlic have softened, add the chicken pieces and cook for approx 2-3 minutes until the chicken starts to colour.

Now add the chillies, tomatoes, tomato purée, and begin to stir in the pre-prepared Vindaloo paste. Add salt and pepper to taste, and bring to the boil. Once boiling, lower the heat and simmer whilst stirring occasionally for approx 1 hour. During this period, it's important not to let the chicken Vindaloo dry out, so add a ½ cup of water as necessary. Add more chilli powder according to your taste.

LO MAI CHI
(from Chapter 4)

Mom usually makes this recipe in her spare time in the afternoon. This is always a surprise to come home to!

Ingredients

Makes around 15-20 pieces.

Ingredients for the wrapper
1 cup rice flour
¾ cup glutinous rice flour
3 tbsp sugar
1½ cup water
Ingredients for the filling
1¼ cup peanuts (roasted and crushed)
5 tbsp granulated sugar

Method

Bake the rice flour for 45 minutes at 250°F and stirring every 10 minutes. Set it aside to cool.

Mix water and sugar. Pour into the glutinous rice flour and mix. Grease a tray. Pour glutinous mixture into the tray. Steam for ½ hour or until cooked. Set it aside to cool.

Pour the cooked glutinous rice dough into the roasted rice flour. Cut into small portions and flatten each dough.

In separate bowl, mix peanuts and granulated sugar together to create the filling. Fill the dough with the filling and seal the dough. Coat with the roasted rice flour and serve.

HOMESTYLE CHANKO-NABE
(from Chapter 6)

A hot and healthy meal usually made by Mom during the cold winter months.

Ingredients

350 grams chicken thigh/breast meat
1 block soft tofu
½ head Chinese cabbage
3 stalks Japanese leek
2 onions
1 carrot
1 pack shimeji mushrooms
1 pack king oyster mushrooms
2 pieces aburaage (remove excess oil)
1000 ml water
3 tbsp Chinese chicken stock powder
1 tsp salt
8 cloves grated garlic
1 tbsp grated ginger

Method

Cut the ingredients into pieces small enough that they will cook easily.

Add water, Chinese chicken stock powder, salt, garlic, and ginger in the pot and heat. Add the Chinese cabbage and onions to the pot and place all the other ingredients except for the tofu on top.

Allow vegetables to soften and wilt.

Cover with lid and turn to high heat. When it comes to a boil, open the lid just enough so it won't boil over. Turn the heat down to low. While it's simmering, occasionally spoon the broth over everything.

When all the ingredients have cooked through, add the soft tofu, bring to a simmer, and it's done!

MOCHIKO CUPCAKE
(from Chapter 8)

A childhood favorite snack among my siblings and me.

Ingredients

1 box of Mochiko sweet rice flour
1 can of coconut milk
6 tsp sugar

Method

Place Mochiko sweet rice flour, coconut milk, and sugar in large bowl. Mix ingredients together until mixture shows a glutinous consistency. Pour mixture into small microwavable cup moulds and microwave on high for 6-8 minutes. Let cupcakes cool for 5 minutes before serving.

OATMEAL COOKIES
(from Conclusion)

A deceivingly healthy cookie you won't feeling guilty eating.

Ingredients

1 tbsp water
3 tbsp room temperature butter
½ cup brown sugar
¼ cup honey
1 egg
½ cup whole wheat flour
¼ tsp baking soda
1 cup rolled oats
½ cup ground flax seed
½ cup chopped walnuts
Pinch of salt

Method

Preheat oven to 350ºF. Mix together butter, brown sugar, honey, egg, and water thoroughly.

Sift in wheat flour, baking soda, and salt. Add oats, ground flax seed, and walnuts together and mix well. Scoop heaping teaspoonfuls of mixture onto cookie sheet. Place in oven and bake for 15-20 minutes.

Cool on wire rack and serve.

APPENDIX

Education

IBD University: *Education.investors.com*

- Easy learning from IBD
- Explains the basics of investing from how to read stock charts to giving time-saving routines
- Free unless otherwise specified

Investopedia: *www.investopedia.com*

- Has hands-on exercises
- Features video tutorials that breaks down complex investing concepts
- Has a stock simulator for you to test how well you would do in the real markets risk free

Virtual Stock Exchange (VSE): *http://www.marketwatch.com/game/*

- Site created by Market Watch
- Invest stocks in real-time using your virtual portfolio
- Improve on your strategies by creating custom games, joining discussion groups, and much more

More Screeners

MSN: *www.msn.com/en-us/money/stockscreener*

- Free, easy to read charts and data
- User-friendly interface
- buildable and customizable watch lists

US News & World Report: *http://money.usnews.com/investing*

- User-friendly site
- Free, detailed screener for analysis
- Easy navigation to stocks and ETFs

Stock Charts: *Stockcharts.com*

- "Simply the world's best financial charts"
- Offers powerful analytical tools and highly customizable watch lists for the experienced investor
- Real-time chart prices
- $50+/month membership

Company Profiles and News

USA: *www.msn.com/en-us/money*
Canada: *www.msn.com/en-ca/money*
Worldwide Bloomberg: *www.bloomberg.com*

ACKNOWLEDGEMENT

A deep and resounding thank you to the following individuals and organizations for their contribution to this book:

Jacob Chapman, Sazze Partners, Managing Partner, San Jose, California

Ryan T. O'Donnell, Chief Financial Officer at The O'Donnell Group, Chico, California

Timothy W. Holt, Investment Advisor Representative, The Holt Capital Management Group, LLC, Glendale, Arizona

David Bickerton, Portfolio manager at MDH Investment Management, Inc., East Liverpool, Ohio

Trevor Ewen, partner at Neosavvy, New York City, New York

Peter L. Brooks, President of Brooksie Portfolio Management Advisors, Inc., New York City, New York

Tom Weary, Chief Investment Officer of Lau Associates, LLC, Greenville, Delaware

Greg Farrall, President and CEO of Farrall Wealth, Valparaiso, Indiana

Salvatore Buscemi, Managing Director at Dandrew Partners, LLC, New York City, New York

Jason Hilliard, President and Chief Investment Officer at Forecast Capital Management, LLC, Denver, Colorado

Patrick Chiu, Adrian Chan, Sheg Chiu, Ebimayo Studios, Peter Chan, Miladinka Milic, Colin Chik, Vasco Vieira Ribeiro, Bella Bu.

And everyone else who made this book possible ... you know who you are.

INDEX

A

action targets 198, 199, 201, 203, 204
advantages 40
advisors 32, 35, 141, 145
a plan 47, 52, 58, 68, 77, 78, 79, 80, 85, 88, 93, 109, 139, 147, 161, 167, 174, 175, 176, 187, 207
April Fool's 112
Asia Crisis 108
AutoCanada 6
automated 188, 189, 207
averages 42, 47, 99

B

banks 4, 39, 50, 124, 186, 195
Barron's 27
Berlin 105, 106
best in class 120, 127, 129
Bickerton, David 38, 81, 169, 227
Big Hero 6 62
Black Monday 107
Bloomberg 83, 112, 194, 226
blue chip 5, 127, 130, 183, 185, 203
Bob 103, 104
Bogle, John 57
Bombardier 5
Bonaparte, Napoleon 31
borrow 66, 102, 103, 152, 163, 164, 172
Bristol-Myers Squibb Co. 6
broker 30, 32, 33, 34, 35, 36, 38, 43, 47, 50, 58, 66, 207
brokers 32, 33, 34, 35, 43, 52, 56, 70, 87, 101, 127
Brookfield Infrastructure Partners 6
Brooks, Peter L. 92, 120, 227

Buffett, Warren 50, 81, 129, 167, 208
Buscemi, Salvatore 122, 147, 227

C

Canada iv, 2, 3, 17, 38, 39, 40, 50, 54, 89, 101, 102, 162, 197, 226
Canada Savings Bonds 17
Canadian National Railway Company 153
Carlson, Ben 103
Carrick, Rob 25
cash on hand 168, 169, 172, 186
Castro 106
catalyst 64, 66
challenge 30, 55, 72, 79, 82, 92, 113, 119, 136, 141, 157, 159, 172, 173, 177
Chan, Adrian 170, 228
Chanko-nabe 116, 117, 119, 136, 218
Chapman, Jacob 124, 227
Chernobyl 107
Chevron 27, 231
China VOIP & Digital 4
CNN 24, 144
Coach 139, 140, 163, 186
Coca-Cola 27, 231
Coke 98
Cold War 105
common sense x, 2, 49, 53, 54, 55, 56, 58, 65, 79, 123, 129, 167, 181, 203, 206
compound interest 135
crash 25, 27, 81, 89, 91, 92, 93, 101, 103, 106, 107, 108
Cuban Missile Crisis 106
cyclical 126, 195

D

Dad 2, 3
Dalbar's 86
de Bono, Edward 191
Debt Crisis 107
decisions x, 8, 34, 52, 54, 60, 62, 63, 79, 87, 143, 145, 148, 149, 165, 174, 189, 204, 206, 207
deflation 99, 100
Dell ix
derailments 153, 155
discipline 2, 3, 13, 42, 47, 62, 63, 68, 70, 73, 74, 75, 77, 79, 80, 84, 88, 91, 92, 95, 96, 109, 116, 139, 140, 186, 192, 208
diversification 38, 116, 117, 142
diversify 116, 117, 118, 127, 162, 165, 174, 195, 197
dividends 6, 27, 38, 41, 69, 100, 127, 130, 131, 132, 135, 142, 146, 157, 162, 163, 164, 165, 166, 168, 174, 176, 180, 185, 190, 194, 196, 197
doing the opposite 81, 93
Dot Com Crash 26
Dow (DJIA) 7, 26, 27, 28, 29, 50, 105, 106, 107, 108, 109, 155
DuPont 27, 231

E

Einstein, Albert 159
Eisenhower, Dwight D. 105
Electronically Traded Funds (ETFs) 38
emotions x, 10, 15, 52, 70, 79, 80, 82, 84, 85, 87, 88, 91, 110, 111, 167, 187, 201, 204, 206
Enbridge 5, 50
enemy 57, 150, 158
energy 5, 6, 125, 170, 191
Entry/exit 139
Ewen, Trevor 181, 227
exit strategy 139, 140, 142

F

Facebook 148
facts x, 10, 15, 42, 47, 51, 54, 62, 63, 65, 77, 82, 109, 110, 145, 146, 147, 150, 157, 158, 166, 182, 187, 203, 204, 207
Farrall, Greg 110, 129, 151, 227
fees 29, 34, 35, 37, 38, 40, 44, 45, 47, 50, 56, 76, 168, 194, 199
Ferriss, Timothy 156
Financial Crisis 26
financial groupies 26, 39, 59, 65, 105, 106, 107, 108, 148
Findley, John 146, 150
food ix, 1, 68, 118, 119, 125, 127, 162, 163, 168, 169, 195
Ford 129, 145, 146, 147, 150
Fukushima 108
fundamentals 65, 80, 91, 124, 145, 146, 147, 148, 153, 181, 182
future 60, 61, 62, 63, 64, 99, 125, 147, 181

G

gambling 42, 43, 58, 64, 103, 128, 163, 177
General Patton, George 81
Goetzmann, William 89
Graham, Benjamin 9
Great Crash 26, 27
Great Depression 27, 41, 59, 97, 100, 105, 106, 107, 129, 131
Great-West Life 50
Gretzky, Wayne 79, 145
growth 5, 6, 33, 38, 107, 130, 138, 156, 164, 174
Guang Zhou Global Telecom Inc. 4
Gulf of Tonkin Incident 106

H

Harvard 45
healthcare 68, 126
Hilliard, Jason 171, 228
Holt, Timothy W. 43, 54, 60, 71, 227
Hong Kong 2
house money 6, 133, 135, 136, 142, 163, 164, 165, 168, 175, 176, 199, 203, 205
Housing bubble 108
Hurricane Andrew 107
Hurricane Sandy 108

INDEX | 231

I

inclusivity 21
inflation 17, 18, 27, 30, 37, 86, 87, 97, 98, 99, 100, 104, 117, 132, 177, 185
infrastructure 6, 126, 163
Instagram 148
Investment Retirement Account (IRA) 40

J

Jacks, Evelyn 17
Jerod 81
Joel, Billy 150
Jordan, Michael 79
Jorion, Philippe 89

K

Kennedy, John F. 97, 106
Khmer Rouge 106
Korean War 105
Kraft 129

L

law of probability 76, 77
leeching 38
Lichello, Robert 143
liquidity 22, 32
Loblaws 50
logic 79, 122, 192
Lo Mai Chi 74, 75, 77, 86, 87, 92, 95, 136, 216
lower profits 41
low maintenance 29
luck 7, 42, 58, 62, 75, 78, 79, 88, 91

M

Mabcure Inc. 4
Macdonald's 98
Magna International 6
management expense ratio 37
Manulife 6, 50
media 5, 49, 50, 51, 66, 83, 112, 144, 145, 147, 148, 149, 150, 151, 152, 156, 157, 158, 159, 181
Merck & Co. 6

MetLife Inc 6
Microsoft. Nike. Coca-Cola. DuPont. Chevron. Visa. Walmart. Proctor & Gamble. 27
Mochiko cupcake 160
money work for you 30
Monopoly 78
movement 26, 110, 126, 185, 197
movements 9, 79, 111, 148, 197, 204
multi-level marketing 15
mutual funds 34, 36, 37, 38, 40, 43, 44, 45, 50, 52, 86, 87, 99, 101, 109, 110, 117, 169

N

Newark Race Riots 106
New York Stock Exchange (NYSE) 7
New York Times 151
Nicklaus, Jack 79
Nieves, Brian 148, 149
Nike 27, 231
noise 51, 52, 148, 152, 156, 157
non-cyclical 126
Nortel 101, 102, 163
North Korea 106, 108

O

oatmeal cookies 205
O'Donnell, Ryan T. 20, 111, 116, 227
OPEC 106
opinions 49, 51, 64, 144, 145, 146, 148, 149, 150, 158, 182
Orman, Suze 120
own advice 51, 52
Oxford 61

P

patience 21, 70, 71, 75, 116, 185
Pearl Harbour 105
Pembina Pipeline Corp 5
penny stocks 4, 5, 21, 51, 52, 127, 128, 132
permanent 48, 89, 147
pharmaceuticals 6, 126
physics 96
Polaroid Corporation 204

portfolio 6, 32, 50, 88, 99, 103, 122, 123, 127, 128, 135, 148, 162, 164, 165, 168, 173, 174, 186, 194, 195, 196, 198, 225
predict 9, 47, 61, 72, 80, 110, 111, 113, 118, 204
Proctor and Gamble 129

Q

quality companies 68, 122, 195
Quantitative Analysis of Investor Behaviour (QAIB) 86, 87
Quantum Fund 61

R

real estate 12, 18, 21, 22, 24, 25, 29, 32, 39, 98, 118, 125, 133, 162, 181
real world 139, 142
recipes x, 8, 119, 209
Rediff 5
reinvesting 6
reserves 179, 186, 187, 189, 190
Rockefeller, John D. 131, 149
Rogers Communications 50
Rogers, Jimmy 57, 61, 88, 231
Royal Bank 4

S

SARS 108
scalability 23
scammers 34, 45, 51
ScotiaBank 4
sectors 6, 117, 120, 122, 123, 124, 127, 129, 162, 165, 194, 195, 196, 198
shopping list 192, 194, 195, 197, 198
Shoven, John B. 29
Siegel, Jeremy 27
Soros, George 61, 80
S&P 103, 104
spaghetti 31, 32, 34, 36, 45, 50, 53, 211, 212
Sputnik 106
Stanford 29
Starbucks 141
stress 20, 29, 60, 66, 67, 68, 69, 70, 72, 74, 118, 152, 157, 207

Sub-prime mortgage crisis 108
Suez Crisis 106
Suncor Energy Inc 5
Sun Life Financial Inc 6
survival tools 115, 116

T

Tax-Free Savings Account (TFSA) 38, 39, 133
TD Bank 4
technology 45, 112, 126, 127, 195
temporary 5, 41, 48, 66, 148, 179, 181, 182, 184
Ten Commandments 159, 160, 168
Tesla 112, 113
The Globe and Mail 25, 194, 196
The Goldman Sachs Group 155
The Hustler 62
throne-room traders 66
timing 64, 66, 72, 74, 80, 103, 110, 143
tipping 83
Toronto Stock Exchange (TSX) 101
Toyota Motor Corporation 153
traders 29, 33, 59, 61, 64, 67, 68, 69, 72, 74, 113, 153, 166, 188, 206
trading x, 33, 39, 43, 59, 60, 61, 63, 64, 66, 68, 69, 74, 76, 80, 89, 112, 113, 146, 152, 153, 166, 194, 199
transportation 6, 117, 163, 186
Trump, Donald 20, 122
Tuchman, Mitchell 45
Twain, Mark 95
Twitter iv, 148

U

universal truths 96, 97, 113, 119
University of California 89
USA Today 151
USSR 105, 106
utilities 125, 186

V

Vindaloo chicken 57, 68, 213
Visa 27, 231
volatility 80

W

Walmart 27, 231
Weary, Tom 29, 87, 227
Wharton 27
Who Wants to be a Millionaire? 149
women 69, 70, 71, 75, 81, 82, 120, 170
wontons 8, 11, 12, 209, 210
Woody, Allen 205
World Trade Center 107, 108

Y

Y2K 108
Yale 61, 89
Yale School of Management 89

Z

zero 79, 101, 102, 114, 115, 127, 144, 157, 163, 164

CPSIA information can be obtained
at www.ICGtesting.com
Printed in the USA
LVOW07*1433180517
535008LV00009B/155/P

9 780994 911506